D1566337

CHILDREN AND THE WORLD WIDE WEB

CHILDREN AND THE WORLD WIDE WEB

Tool or Trap?

Samuel Joshua Friedman

University Press of America,® Inc.
Lanham · New York · Oxford

Copyright © 2000 by
Samuel Joshua Friedman

University Press of America,® Inc.
4720 Boston Way
Lanham. Maryland 20706

12 Hid's Copse Rd.
Cumnor Hill, Oxford OX2 9JJ

Library of Congress Cataloging-in-Publication Data

Friedman. Samuel Joshua.
Children of the World Wide Web : tool or trap? /
Samuel Joshua Friedman.
p.   cm.
Includes bibliographical references and index.
1.   Internet and children. 2. World Wide Web—Social aspects.
3. Internet—Censorship.
HQ784.I58F75   2000   303.48'33—dc21   00-061580 CIP

ISBN 0-7618-1824-3 (cloth: alk. ppr.)

Contents

Acknowledgements

There are a number of people I wish to thank for contributing to this book. First, my thanks to Professors Howard Budin, Hope Leichter, and Robert McLintock for their participation in my doctoral defense committee. My thanks go out to Prof. Robert Taylor whose thoughts and insights have helped me significantly in writing this book. To Issac Hershkowitz, a friend and fellow student, who supported my efforts in many ways despite my oft-felt frustrations. To Janet Hulstrand, for helping me adapt my dissertation and preparing it for publication. And I wish to acknowledge and thank my best friend, Professor James Roman, without whom this document could never have been written.

This book is dedicated to my parents, Wolf and Miriam Friedman. I am truly grateful to my father, whose memory and presence continues to fill me every day. And to my mother for her love and the many sacrifices she has made to make certain that my life and endeavors would result in a better experience than her own.

Finally, this book is dedicated to the survivors of Hitler's extermination camps, and to The Second Generation for their struggle to lead a better life.

S. J. F.

Introduction

Recent growth on the Internet can only be described as explosive. In 1989 there were about 1,000 host computers connected to the Internet. In 1997, there were approximately 4,000,000. (Street, 1997, p. 27). It is currently estimated that more than 50% of American households have a computer, or have access to one at their place of work.

As a result of this new technology, mass culture is being reshaped. In the 1960's, Marshall McLuhan argued that "the medium is the message," that the contents of any culture cannot be abstracted from the technologies through which those contents are produced, conveyed, and preserved. And as the information revolution continues, it seems that McLuhan was right. Even if the words are identical, a message sent by e-mail is different than one sent via surface mail, and a conversation over the telephone is qualitatively different from one conducted in person. The film I watch on my VCR is not the 'same' as it was when I saw it in the movie theater, and so on.

The phenomenal growth of this new information and communications medium is nothing short of revolutionary. And as the explosive growth continues, complicated new questions about how to handle it are being raised.

Among other matters of concern, a number of factors have made targeting children on the Internet both compelling and practical for advertisers. The first and most obvious point is that children comprise a significant and powerful consumer group. In 1995, children under the age of twelve spent $14 billion dollars, teenagers spent another $67 billion, and together they influenced $160 billion of their parents' spending. Second, more and more children are going online. According to

Jupiter Publications, publishers of *Digital Kids Report,* in 1997 nearly 1 million kids were using the Web and at least 3.8 million had access. These figures are quadrupling every four years, and these statistics have caught the attention of nearly every company that targets children.

Unlike television, radio and print mediums, the Internet is generally free of government regulation. The Computer Decency Act of the Telecommunications Act of 1996 was an attempt to regulate the content of the Internet, but a U.S. District Court declared it unconstitutional, and a violation of free speech. The judge involved in the decision commented that the Internet is the greatest example of free speech the world has ever known.

The recent history of technological improvements is also the history of the invasion of privacy, and the Internet has presented unprecedented opportunities for those who would invade our privacy. It is a powerful interactive medium that allows advertisers to have one-on-one communication with consumers and establish personal relationships with them. As it takes hold, throughout the online world, the commercial imperative threatens to undermine the potential social, educational, and cultural benefits of this new medium. The interactivity it offers is especially appealing to children and to their imagination and fantasies, and because it is so enticing it renders them more than ever vulnerable to unscrupulous attempts to gain their loyalty, their dollars and to take advantage of their innocence and immaturity. Children naturally tend to be trusting and vulnerable to psychological manipulation. Advertisers know this and are not about to miss an opportunity to take advantage of it.

The computer age has also created a new generation gap: many children are allowed to explore the World Wide Web without parental supervision and monitoring. Children generally have a better aptitude and temperament for new technologies, and companies are using children in their product development efforts, for example, in the area of computer games. Finally, as an advertising medium, the Internet is relatively inexpensive compared to broadcast and print media.

All of these factors present companies with an affordable, practical, and unregulated medium possessing technologies that enable them to communicate and interact one-on-one with a very significant, trusting, and vulnerable consumer group. This presents an atmosphere ripe for abuse, exploitation, and manipulation of the consumer.

This situation leads naturally to several conclusions: the most important is that children, despite the fact that they possess the aptitude and ability to use new technologies effectively, are still children. They need the maturity, wisdom, and guidance of adults. They need to learn to distinguish right from wrong, and to be protected from anyone who might exploit, manipulate, and use them while they are learning. They also need to be shielded from commercialism and greed, so that they can have a childhood that doesn't rush them into the world of adults prematurely, before they are prepared for it.

At the present time, because of the lack of regulation, online advertisers are getting away with practices that they could not in print or in broadcasting media. There are currently no safeguards available to ensure that children will be protected from these practices. The industry claims that voluntary self-regulation is the answer: but it is hard to imagine, given the evidence of the past, that this is a sufficient answer to the complicated dilemmas posed by this new medium.

Regulators have been dazzled by the seemingly transformative powers of the Internet as a new communications technology to the extent that the traditions of broadcasting policy are being transformed as well. And despite the interventions of many "public-interest' groups, existing community media models are not being utilized.

The Internet is a medium, like any other, that develops within a social and political environment. Much of Internet discourse tends to abstract technology from society and place its development in a separate sphere, isolated from the surrounding culture. This is a danger that may lead to a limiting of choice, or rather that the choices we can make will be meaningless. How many of us have forty or fifty channels to choose from on cable television, and how many of these choices are good ones? The commercialization of the Internet is not bad in and of itself, but the possibility that commercial interests can dominate the Internet so that there will be fewer meaningful choices, is something to be concerned about.

The choices before us involve the methods of ownership, as well as matters of decision-making and financing, not just individual programming or the types of programming permitted. The history of radio, which was much more diverse in its infancy in the 1920s, shows us that it is possible to go from a state of greater diversity to one of lesser diversity. The issue is not based on the marketplace at work and consumer choice, but of effective commercial lobbying of lawmakers. The technology or culture of the Internet cannot protect it from government regulation or commercialization. The Internet is dependent on users: they have the power to intervene politically in a manner that creates a medium that reflects our need for choice and the free flow of information and opinion.

David Britt (1995), chief executive of the Children's Television Workshop and the producer of "Sesame Street" on public television, acknowledges the power of online communications, but he expresses considerable doubt about the ultimate disposition of that power. He says,

> We have to recognize that children are going to learn from online whether its something we think is educational or not. Like television, it's not a question of whether children are going to learn; it's only a question of what they are going to learn. When we do it wrong, with violence or with mayhem or with completely mindless entertainment, they are going to learn from that. And some of them will be harmed. When we do it right, children will learn some things that will help them grow and become better citizens. It's a real and powerful responsibility. (n.p.).

Technological solutions promise some help to parents in controlling what their children see, but these efforts have been concerned more with screening out isolated pockets of sex and violence than with confronting the much more subtle and pervasive problem of online advertising. Given the corporate sector's track record and its current Web and online performance, industry self-regulation is also an inadequate option. In fact, unless there are carefully considered policies, it is unlikely that effective safeguards will be created to protect children from advertisers.

Nonetheless, what is intriguing about the Internet, and one cause for optimism, is that it is still a work in progress. Traffic laws for the "Information Superhighway" haven't been written yet. If the multimedia junk mail that Kellogg's, Frito-Lay, Disney, Fox, and so many others are churning out gives us some second thought, it may be still possible to limit such abuses.

There is no question that a protocol of content regulations is problematic, and that attempting to regulate media challenges some of the most cherished precepts in our Constitution. But it is also important to protect America's children and its future. How will we deal with this issue as a new medium takes hold? How do we reconcile the protection of our children's rights without infringing on the First Amendment rights of American adults? There is nothing simple about this question, and the answer won't come easily.

While freedom of expression is an absolute construct of our democracy, with serious implications for the Internet, a discussion of access and the publication of ideas are often associated with commercial imperatives. And though providing equal access to the technology of the Internet to all children is an essential component for democratizing the World Wide Web, commercial interests have a profound influence on children and will control and dominate a child's use of the Web. Advertising plays an important role in the relationship between the Web and children, and unfortunately, the welfare of children is subordinate to the commercial imperative.

This book attempts to provide food for thought on these important issues by looking to the past for models on how to approach them, and by raising questions about how we might use the Internet to improve rather than impoverish or contaminate our future. As a tool for advertising to children, the Web involves thinking in new and creative ways. It is up to us to build this medium collectively, in a way that allows for us, our children, and our future to be ultimately enriched.

CHAPTER 1

The History of Regulation

While the Internet is raising new questions, the regulation of mass communication has always been an issue for society. Societal and cultural pressures have predicated the need for regulatory laws, and establishing such laws has been within the role of government. Indeed, creating a protocol of oversight pertaining to children has been an area where special interest groups have effectively lobbied in the past.

MORALITY AND THE MOVIES

The Motion Picture Producers and Distributors Association initiated the concept of a rating system in the early 1900's. During the 1920's, as the motion picture industry began to grow rapidly, many religious and civic leaders concluded that movies would cause a "deterioration of moral norms and harmful political changes to American life" (Defleur, 1996, p. 174). People believed that "the new medium was negatively influencing children and teaching them unwholesome ideas" (p. 174).

Fear of stronger government regulation led the movie industry to impose a self-regulatory system. In order to implement this system, Will Hays, a former postmaster general, was appointed to head their organization. Hays initiated a morality clause, which stated that if an actor was caught in an immoral situation, he could be dropped from his contract. In addition, Hays wrote a set of guidelines, otherwise known as the "production code" which "restricted depictions of sex" in movies (Defleur, 1996, p. 175). Movies now began to avoid any direct treatment of sexual themes and sexual behavior.

THE LEGION OF DECENCY

In addition to Hays's production code, many private organizations became involved in censoring films. The Legion of Decency, which was formed by the American bishops of the Roman Catholic Church in 1936, developed a list of recommended and non-recommended films and distributed the list to Catholics as well as to the general public. Currently, the Legion of Decency has been replaced by the Catholic Church's Office for Film and Broadcasting. This group remains active and continues to promote their own rating system for movies, though its voice is not nearly as powerful as it was in the 1930s and 1940s.

The Legion of Decency aimed to combat immoral movies. People took a pledge promising never to go to any morally objectionable movie or any movie theater that had ever shown a morally objectionable film. The Legion's ratings were very strict: *The Miracle on 34th Street,* for instance, now a cherished Christmas classic, featured a divorced woman, thereby earning a B rating from the Legion of Decency for being morally objectionable in part. Nevertheless, the Legion of Decency was very effective in discouraging Hollywood from making movies that would earn their disapproval. During that time, Catholics were a powerful force to be reckoned with by the movie industry.

When it began, both Hollywood and Catholics took the ratings seriously. Movie producers attempted to keep their movies acceptable to the Legion of Decency, knowing that a "condemned" or "C" classification would deal a blow to box office receipts. In those days, lists of movies and their Legion of Decency codes were even posted in the vestibules of churches.

The Legion of Decency's influence waned when television became a household fixture, though, changing people's entertainment needs. As accessibility became so much easier, prohibition became more difficult. Family entertainment, once Hollywood's main draw to the movie theater now came right into people's living rooms. In response, Hollywood began to pursue more adult themes. Actresses such as Jane Russell brought cleavage to the screen and dollars to the box office.

At the same time, fewer priests continued to display Legion of Decency ratings in church. Society was changing, and so were people's opinions of what was acceptable. The bishops reacted to these on-screen changes by adding more ratings to the Legion of Decency codes, taking into account the growing media savvy of adult audiences. But that still wasn't enough. The Legion of Decency could no longer interest the educated Catholic population with a mere classification. As a result, the bishops decided that "no film would be classified without a review or at least an accompanying capsule review." The Legion wanted to continue to provide a service, and to let people know what a movie was about by providing a summary of a movie. (See Appendix I)

Things began to change toward the end of the 1950's. In 1957, Pope Pius XII issued an encyclical (*Miranda Prorsus*) that called for the Legion of Decency to be more positive and to put its emphasis on promoting good movies rather than condemning bad ones. In response to that encyclical, the Legion of Decency changed and the pledge gradually faded out of use, until it was finally completely forgotten. By 1975, the Legion of Decency ceased to exist and was replaced by the Bishops' new Catholic rating system. That essentially ended the Church's influence on the movie industry. The Legion of Decency was eventually replaced by the rating system we now have.

In addition, the Supreme Court rejected legal movie censorship beginning in the 1950's. Following the demise of the Hays Production Code, various public groups emerged as media watchdogs, replacing nearly all other sources of control.

Responding to explicit violence against women, negative stereotypes of gay and lesbian images, 'racist' representations, and 'blasphemous' interpretations of the *Bible,* groups from both the Left and Right staged protests in front of theaters and boycotted movie studios. The New Censors showed how groups on the Left empowered by social movements in the 1960's, and groups on the Right propelled by the successes of the New Christian Right and 'The Moral Majority,' have used similar strategies in attempting to control movie content" (Lyons, 1998, n.p.).

Although some of the early attempts at monitoring and influencing Hollywood productions may seem excessive or overly authoritative now, perhaps the impulse to curb the instinct of producers to go for "the lowest common denominator" was not a bad one. Though today it is hardly possible to think of our lives without the movies, and most Americans cringe at the thought of censorship, many of us are also concerned about the ill effects of the violence and other negative influences found in so many Hollywood productions, and especially about its effect on our children.

REGULATING BROADCASTING:
THE FEDERAL COMMUNICATIONS COMMISSION

Regulation of the broadcast industry was placed in the hands of the FCC by means of the 1934 Federal Communications Act. The use of regulations was based on the assumption that broadcasters used valuable public resources that should serve the public interest. Initially this involved radio and telephone communications. Later, broadcast television was added.

The 'Radio Act of 1927,' the forerunner of the 1934 Act, was passed by Congress to bring order to radio broadcasting and regulate the media. This law asserted that the airwaves belong to the public and that broadcasters must operate in "the public interest" at all times. An independent agency, the Federal Radio Commission, was also established to supervise the regulation of broadcasting. When it became evident that the radio industries, as well as the telephone and telegraph industry were interdependent, President Roosevelt initiated the Federal Communications Act of 1934. This law established basic philosophical principles stating that the airways are public property and that commercial broadcasters are licensed to use the airwaves. The main condition for use of the airwaves was whether the broadcaster served 'the public interest, convenience, and necessity." To enforce the Federal Communications Act, the Federal Communications Commission (or FCC) was created and was given the power to make rules and regulations within the broad framework of the Act. The FCC carried the full weight of the law, which has been frequently amended since then and stands as the basic regulation of the broadcast industry to this day.

In 1949, the FCC adopted the Fairness Doctrine, which made broadcasters responsible for seeking out and presenting all sides of an issue when controversial issues were covered. This later was applied to cigarette commercials where broadcasters had to give equal airtime to ads denouncing smoking.

On August 8, 1996, the FCC passed new regulations designed to clarify commercial broadcasters' obligations for the educational and informational needs of children. Commission documents argued that such an order was necessary because (a) the language of the Children's Television Act of 1990 was not precise and led to variations in the way broadcasters complied with the Act; (b) broadcasters were claiming to satisfy their obligations to the child audience with programs that could not be reasonably viewed as "specifically designed" to educate and inform children; and (c) parents and others did not have the information they needed about the broadcasters' efforts in order to provide timely feedback to the broadcaster and other regulatory agencies. In January 1997 these new regulations took effect and broadcasters were required to start identifying their educational offerings to the viewing public. In addition, beginning in September 1998, broadcasters seeking to expedite a review of their license renewal applications were told that they would need to air at least three hours a week of core educational programming for children.

Meanwhile, during the 1980's, a competing philosophy based on free market theories had begun to dominate the U.S. Congress and regulatory agencies. In the past decade, broadcasting and the telecommunications industry has seen substantial deregulation, including the Telecommunications Act of 1996.

Today, the FCC is still guided by the Federal Communications Act of 1934 as well as the Telecommunications Act of 1996. The Agency is responsible for making rules and regulations within the framework of the original act and carries the force of law. The 1934 law was very specific on some matters such as regulations concerning the use of broadcast media by political candidates. It was vague on issues such as the mandate that broadcasters operate their stations in "the public interest, convenience or necessity" since this could have a wide area of interpretation. As a result, the FCC has and continues to develop many rules and policies in order to implement the public interest requirement

The growth of communications and broadcasting technology has stimulated the growth of regulation of new industries. As the technology advances and as cultural and social mores develop and change, this has become an ongoing process. Today, regulation of the Internet has become a sensitive issue and the FCC continues to look into this topic. However, due to its nature as a 'personal' communication tool and its international reach, its regulation is proving to be difficult and controversial.

RADIO AND OTHER TECHNOLOGIES: A PARALLEL WITH THE INTERNET

The history of radio technology has had a strong impact on the evolution of broadcast regulation. In the early 1920's, as radio began to grow as a mass medium, "the battle for more frequency space and less channel interference intensified" (Campbell, 1998, p. 101). Radio was in a state of chaos. During this time, there were no regulations to restrict the amount of stations broadcasting over the airwaves. This led to clogged airwaves, poor reception, and a sharp decline of the sale of radio sets.

In order to restore 'order to the airwaves,' Secretary of Commerce, Herbert Hoover, ordered radio stations "to share time and to set aside certain frequencies for entertainment, news, sports, and weather" (Campbell, 1998, p. 101). As one station challenged Hoover and deliberately jammed the airwaves, the courts decided that Hoover had the power to grant licenses, not to restrict stations from operating. This helped to establish the Radio Act of 1927. Congress had passed this Act to enforce that "licensees did not own their channels but could license them as long as they operated in the public interest, convenience, or necessity" (p. 101). To reinforce this act and to continue to negotiate channel problems, the 1927 act created the Federal Radio Commission (or FRC). This agency eventually became the FCC, which soon became a powerful regulatory agency, covering radio and telephone, and eventually television, cable and the Internet.

Besides restoring order to the airwaves, regulating radio had also encompassed some political aspirations. Initially, the Navy had tried to control wireless telegraphy by "controlling the manufacture of radio transmitters and receivers" (Campbell, 1998, p. 101). However, the "auctioning of the airwaves" had soon become a fast revenue stream for commercial interests. In 1925, Herbert Hoover had stated, "four years ago we were dealing with a scientific toy; today we are dealing with a vital force in American life" (p. 101). In addition, the attempt by Josephus Daniels, then Secretary of the Navy to control radio, set a precedent for the criticism of government or military oversight of a mass medium. He said," the passage of this bill will secure for all time to the Navy Department the control of radio in the United States, and will enable the Navy to continue the splendid work it has carried out during the war" (Barnouw, 1982, p. 20). Addressing the issue of military control Congressman William S. Greene of Massachusetts said, "I have never heard before that it was necessary for one person to own all the air in order to breathe. Having just won a fight against autocracy, we would start an autocratic movement with this bill" (Barnouw, 1982, p. 21).

Some of the basic issues decided in the course of the regulation of radio have many similarities and parallels to the Internet of today. In its early years, radio was a decentralized technology that allowed amateur broadcasters the ability to present content of interest to either themselves or their community. There were a wide range of institutions and individuals, representing all sectors of society that operated radio stations. In addition, radio equipment was plentiful and inexpensive, and radio expertise was easily accessible.

Today, broadcasting is a major social and commercial institution based on a set of particular social decisions resulting from the use of technology. The Communications Decency provisions of the Telecommunications Act of 1996 have been pivotal in the history of Internet regulations, in the way we look at the Internet, and in what it means.

The Telecommunications Act of 1996 created an overhaul and reform of federal communications policymaking and regulations. The Act relies on increased competition for developing new services and affects the following areas: Radio and Television Broadcasting, Cable Television, Telephone Services, Internet and On-line Computer Services, and Telecommunications Equipment Manufacturing.

The Communications Decency provisions dealt with the degree to which government can regulate the transmission of objectionable material over computer networks, including the Internet. It included measures to shield minors from indecent communications transmitted through telecommunications devices and interactive computer services. According to the Act, it is a crime to knowingly transmit obscene or indecent communications to any recipient under the age of 18. The Act also took measures to create a system of rating video programming for violent, sexual, or other indecent content. It required TV manufacturers to install a "V chip" capable of blocking programs with specified ratings. All newly manufactured television sets are today required to install the chip.

To compare the Internet to early radio is to caution against any belief that the technology of the Internet is radically different from what has come before, in its ability to change the world, and that such change is unstoppable. Today, we no longer think of radio as being a "cutting edge" communications technology. Though we listen to it in our cars, it is not a primary medium for entertainment and information. However, between the late 1920's and the early 1950's, radio was a "hot new medium." The era was called "The Golden Age of Radio" and saw the creation of many genres of programming available on television and cable today. At that time, a mix of commercial, non-commercial, and amateur broadcasters controlled the radio spectrum.

It is difficult to imagine American media today as anything but uniformly commercial. Advertising is the economic engine that drives programming decisions. It sustains the efforts of broadcasters, whether on radio, television, cable, or the Internet. However, in the early years of radio, this was not the case. It was, "a period of experimentation in an attempt to find financially sustainable models for radio broadcasting" (McChesney, 1993, p. 61). Initially, radio was used for wireless telephony, similar to what we would identify as HAM radio operators. Afterwards, the medium was used for other means of broadcasting such as structured news and information. What evolved was a kind of "promotional" broadcasting. Businesses such as department stores and other types of media such as newspapers began radio stations in order to promote themselves. These stations operated at a financial loss.

From a commercial perspective, the 1920's began a search for a business model for broadcasting. Advertising and sponsorship were generally derided as methods of achieving sustainability, as is true today with the Internet. We are attempting to create business models that support the provision of content. However, for many businesses, the Internet is today an extension of existing marketing efforts that offer little immediate prospect of cost recovery.

Many of the democratic elements and the diversity of radio that characterized its infancy did not survive the 1920's. Amateur frequencies were restricted and the very form and ownership of radio was legislated. This ultimately resulted in a limiting of meaningful choice. In the 1920's, radio amateurs saw limits on frequency use. However, there was a general effort to "open up bandwidth for institutional broadcasters" (Rosen, 1980, p. 32). During this period there was a clear and significant opposition by the public to a network-dominated, advertiser supported, broadcasting system. The Radio Act legislated for a broad-casting system was to be almost purely commercial. As a result, the non-profit and independent broadcaster soon faded from the scene. From the 1934 Radio Broadcasting Act to the present, the principles that support a diverse system of broadcasting (including public, commercial and community elements) are no longer present.

The historical precedent of radio raises the question of who owns the airwaves, a question that has profound implications for the Internet and other mass media. A medium that began as a way for the military to conduct sensitive government probes is now a mass medium with a vital impact on American life. Whether or not the Internet will be regulated remains to be seen.

THE FEDERAL TRADE COMMISSION

Creating an agenda for regulatory policy addressing advertising is a part of the protocol of the Federal Trade Commission (FTC). Historically, the FTC has been an advocate for consumers, creating policies that attempt to protect the public from misleading and decep-tive advertising.

The FTC was established in 1914 as the agency with the principal responsibility for the regulation of interstate commerce. Since 1938, the FTC has been given the power to protect the consumer from the use of "false advertisements" and to prevent "unfair or deceptive acts or practices." The FTC has a history of combating deceptive and unfair practices that harm children. Historically, they have helped establish many regulations pertaining to children's advertising. The Commission was given the power to act on commercials on a case by case basis, and to issue broad Trade Rules and Regulations that could restrict or require certain advertising practices. In the past, the FTC has required that many toy companies disclose the size of toys and whether signifi-cant assembly is required. They also have required many direct mar-keting companies to use caution when distributing free products to households. The FTC has also enforced the law that ads "cannot engage children in potentially hazardous activities since children can tend to imitate other children and lack the ability to foresee and avoid dangers" (Starek, 1997, n.p.).

In the 1960's, the government began regulating the tobacco

industry to protect Americans from the effects of tobacco. In 1965, the government passed an Act which required cigarette packaging to carry the warning, "Cigarette Smoking May Be Hazardous to Your Health." The 1965 Act also prohibited states from mandating the placement of any other statement on packs of cigarettes or advertising. In 1969, the government broadened the federal Cigarette Labeling and Advertising Act of 1965 and amended it to state that no requirement or prohibition based on smoking and health should be imposed under State law with respect to the advertising or promotion of any cigarettes. This indicated that there never was a legal challenge against the state regarding a ban or regulation of outdoor tobacco advertising. However, in 1994, Baltimore, Maryland was the first city to prohibit billboards from displaying tobacco and/or alcohol advertisements. The argument came from a complaint that there is a need to protect children from intrusive forms of advertising. Baltimore's bold action triggered similar efforts by Cincinnati, and by cities in Ohio, California, Minnesota and Massachusetts.

The legal issues pertaining to the Internet and censorship were raised in a speech given by FTC Commissioner Roscoe Starek (1997), who cited some concerns regarding marketing and advertising to children. He stated that alcohol advertising posed a First Amendment issue because such advertising to adults is legal. Starek's observation was that such a restriction on alcohol advertising would not survive First Amendment scrutiny.

In the 1970's, the FTC has used the doctrine of unfairness as a tool to restrict children's advertising and this caused considerable opposition from Congress as well as the advertising industry. In 1980, the FTC promoted an Unfairness Policy Statement that described the Commission's injury and public policy criteria and disavowing any independent reliance on whether the challenged conduct was unethical or unscrupulous. Congress had later amended the FTC Act and defined unfairness "to specify that an unfair act or practice is one that causes or is likely to cause substantial injury to consumers that is not reasonably avoidable and is not outweighed by countervailing benefits to consumers or competition" (Starek, 1997, n.p.). As a regulatory agency, the FTC is responsible for protecting consumer rights, paying special attention to the welfare of children. This is evident in the regulatory policy that the FTC has established.

THE FOOD AND DRUG ADMINISTRATION

While the Food and Drug Administration (FDA) does not have legislative powers over advertising per se, it does have a strong influence on the advertising of the products it governs. Therefore any in-depth discussion of advertising would not be complete without some discussion of the FDA, its history, policies, and realm of authority.

The FDA is a public health agency charged with protecting consumers by enforcing the Federal Food, Drug, and Cosmetic Act. Its responsibilities include making sure that foods are pure and wholesome and are produced under sanitary conditions. It is also responsible for making certain that drugs are safe and effective, that cosmetics are made from appropriate ingredients, and that labels and packaging of products are truthful and informative.

Although the FDA was not established until 1931, efforts to regulate foods and drugs in the U.S. began long before that. In the colonies, local food laws were passed to regulate the weight of loaves of bread that were baked commercially. In 1646, the Massachusetts Bay Colony ordered every baker to use a distinct mark for his bread and to keep the weight of the loaves as had been established by law. Laws such as this often reflected the significance of a particular industry to each colony's economy. Massachusetts had laws governing fish. New York had regulations for the beef industry, and Virginia regulated the tobacco industry. In 1785, Massachusetts enacted the nation's first general food law. "Be it therefore enacted", read the act, "that any person selling diseased, corrupted, contagious, or unwholesome provisions, whether for meat or drink..Öshall be punished by fine, imprisonment, standing in the pillory, or one or more of these punishments" (Patrick, 1988), p. 20). Many other states passed similar legislation in the decades that followed.

In the final decade of the 19th century, many cases of adulterated or mislabeled foods were reported. So-called butter was regularly laced with lard, a fat obtained from pigs. Dangerous chemical preservatives such as boric acid were commonly used in many food products. Items labeled "potted chicken" would often contain no chicken whatsoever. As a result of growing agitation by the public, there were nearly 200 legislative measures introduced to Congress between 1880 and 1906 dealing with the adulteration and mislabeling of food. However, not one of these bills was passed by Congress, which refused to support food and drug legislation. According to Dr. Harvey Wiley, the chief chemist of the U.S. Dept. of Agriculture from 1883 to 1912, opposition to federal pure food legislation was threefold. He wrote,

> In the first instance, opposition came from those who thought such legislation an infringement of the police powers of the various states; secondly, it was opposed by those who failed to grasp the serious nature of the problem; and finally, it was fought by interests who saw in it" passage the termination of lucrative business practices (Patrick, 1988, p. 21).

In 1906, Congress passed the Federal Food and Drug Act where it became a federal crime to mislabel or adulterate food, drinks, and drugs intended for interstate commerce. As important as it was, the Pure Food and Drug Act contained many loopholes. For example, it did not have the power to impose fines or penalties. Technological and marketing advances also made the 1906 law obsolete.

The Food and Drug Administration as we know it today was not established until 1931. The public interest in pure food and drugs was later heightened by the Depression, when Americans wanted to make sure that they got true value for every penny spent, especially on essential items such as food and drugs. Today, the FDA bears little resemblance to the organization that was established in 1931. "It currently employs about 8,000 people with a budget of more than $500 million" (Patrick, 1988, p. 51). FDA regulations regarding food packaging and labeling are quite exacting and extensive. Of all the many federal agencies, none affects us on a daily basis more than the FDA.

In 1937, over 100 people died after using a liquid sulfa drug (Elixir Sulfanilamide). A new law, the Federal Food, Drug, and Cosmetic Act (1938) was created that included provisions requiring manufacturers to prove the safety of new drugs to the FDA before putting them on the market. A growth in consumer activism in the 1960s and 1970s resulted in the passage of additional consumer laws.

In recent times, the FDA and the FTC have developed overlapping jurisdiction over the labeling and advertising of goods, drugs and cosmetics. This also includes advertising on the Internet. However, to avoid duplication or inconsistency of their efforts, the agencies have an agreement where the FTC exercises primary responsibility for the regulation of false or deceptive advertising claims for FDA regulated products and the FDA exercises primary jurisdiction over false and misleading labeling of those products (Memorandum of Understanding between FTC and FDA, 1971).

This agreement, signed in 1971, facilitates the exchange of information and coordination of action by the two agencies.

In August of 1996, President Clinton joined forces with the FDA to announce that nicotine is an addictive drug. This had a major affect on tobacco advertising on the Internet. Further, the FDA proposed restricting all "advertising that reaches children." However, the drawback was that the action could violate the First Amendment. In addition, many people questioned if it was appropriate and legal for the government or any federal agency to dictate what products could be advertised, in what manner, as well as where and when. When it came to children, some people argued that the government was attempting to create a "kid proof" exception to the First Amendment.

REGULATING THE INTERNET

As in the early film industry, the issue of morality and children has been a leading factor in the struggle over whether or not to attempt to censor the Internet. One method suggested for regulating content on the Internet has been to implement a rating code system similar to that established for the movie industry. However, the Internet is not transmitted in space, but over telephone lines and "content providers on the Internet are publishers and not broadcasters" (Wallace & Mangan, 1996, p. 74). Any individual on the Internet can be either a sender or a receiver. The textbook definition of the Internet is "the vast central network of high speed telephone lines designed to link and carry computer information worldwide" (Defleur, 1996, p. 34). From this definition, it has proven difficult in interpreting how to regulate the Internet. This has become a controversial matter since regulation borderlines on creating censorship. The combination of different social and cultural mores prevailing in today's climate, the complexity of the Internet itself, and its method of transmission all add to the difficulty in regulating Internet content.

Numerous legal issues impact upon a protocol of content regulations. There is no question that it is important to protect America's future and its children. But the issues involved address some of the most cherished precepts in the Constitution. One of the key dilemmas is to find a way of reconciling the protection of children's rights without infringing on the rights of American adults.

THE FIRST AMENDMENT AND THE INTERNET

As the media continues to expand its role into the area of communication technology, the government's control of media regulation and oversight of First Amendment protection has also grown. Historically, the relationship between the press and government has been a strained one. The history of the Constitution combined with the history of the press has produced a significant change in how we interpret the First Amendment. The First Amendment to the Constitution states, "Congress shall make no law abridging the freedom of speech of the press"; this phrase serves as the foundation for mass communication law. This interpretation has been used by the courts to "breed disputes" caused by changes in the media. "Print and broadcast television have informally defined the constitutional press and have brought the vast majority of press cases to the courts" (Garry, 1996, p. 97). In order to apply the First Amendment to the Internet, we must first look at the development and impact of the Amendment to other areas of media technology. This will be useful in interpreting the development of the Internet as a global form of communication.

In the history of mass communication, the First Amendment has played a vital role in determining how technology will be developed and communicated to a mass audience. The invention of the printing press by Gutenberg helped to establish widespread literacy and increased the spread of new ideas to a mass audience. However, in England, "licensing acts severely limited access to the printing press to a few printers considered 'safe' by the ruling authorities" (Carter et al., 1994, p. 2). So censorship was exposed even in the earliest form of mass communication.

The next area of communication law dealt with seditious libel. Libel by definition is "the defamation of character in written expression" (Campbell, 1998, p. 483). Many colonial publishers were prosecuted for printing stories criticizing public officials. John Peter Zenger, a New York printer who had published articles criticizing a public official was the first to be acquitted by a jury for seditious libel. (Although critical, the facts he published were true.) This case set a precedent for the First Amendment in determining "the right of a democratic press to criticize public officials" (p. 216).

Free expression over the airwaves continues to be an area that is scrutinized. Historically, the freedom to express political views is protected under the First Amendment. However, in the early 1950's, entertainers were blacklisted if they were found to be associated with a Communist party. Senator Joseph McCarthy had led a campaign to rid government and the media of any ties associated with the Communist party. Eventually, the blacklisting ceased. However, "most broadcasters have been trying to free themselves from the government intrusion they once demanded to clear up technical problems and amateur interference" (Campbell, 1998, p. 460).

Currently, radio personality Howard Stern, continues to violate standards granted by the FCC on his radio program. His defense states he is protected under the guarantees of the First Amendment. Nevertheless, the FCC continues to challenge whether he is broadcasting in the public interest.

As the struggle for free expression continues, one area of censorship that remains controversial is book banning. Book banning campaigns have attempted to remove hundreds of books from libraries as well as from the classroom. Of course, many books that were previously banned are now considered to be great works of American literature: *The Scarlet Letter, The Adventures of Huckleberry Finn, Of Mice and Men, The Color Purple,* and *Catcher in the Rye* are just a few examples of controversial books that at one time or another have been banned. Unfortunately, book banning still exists. During the 1980's and 1990's, for example, books that have attempted to explain "alternative or gay lifestyles" have been challenged by parent organizations that consider their use in schools inappropriate.

Bookselling over the Internet has become a lucrative business, and the issue of buying censored books over the Internet has become another area for the courts to decide. Whether the Internet will be defined as publisher, broadcaster, or neither, it has a unique effect on how to interpret the First Amendment as it relates to the media. As society continues to evolve, the question of whether certain books, television shows, compact discs or movies create harm to children will perpetually be scrutinized and challenged under the First Amendment.

The First Amendment was created to prevent federal as well as state governments from instituting prior restraint, thus limiting free expression; including speech and print. This area of First Amendment law has been a determining factor when examining such areas as hate speech, radio broadcasting, and print. As new areas of conflict emerge, so does the interpretation of the First Amendment.

As we move into the 21st century, it is important to address how the convergence of many media technologies and the increased competition among them will affect the way we exchange information. With the future development of the Internet and the legal issues it is raising, we are in a period of dramatic change. The First Amendment will be used as an instrument to define how one can transmit and receive information over the Internet. The Internet, our first truly interactive and global form of communication, is creating a society that is less dependent on "traditional media such as newspapers and television and has turned to "electronic bulletin boards, conferencing services, and computer networks, in order to receive information" (Garry, 1996, p. 10). Examining "the emerging technologies that facilitate interactive communication will provide a rare opportunity to reshape the future course of the First Amendment" (p. 10). With previous First Amendment issues, the focus was in the activities of the press. The constitutional focus will now be on "how society communicates." There was never a need to define the press, since the identity of the press was never an issue. In the past, the press was clearly defined as television, print, and radio media. Future changes in First Amendment doctrines will focus primarily on press identity and on the particular communication services that qualify for constitutional protection. The government will play a "different role in forging First Amendment doctrines" (p. 20). One of the shifts towards redefining the First Amendment as it relates to new communication technology is, "to define the type of press that is immune from government restriction" (p. 21). Not defining the press would result in an increase of unconstitutional regulation. For some of these changes to occur, it has been suggested that "the courts might have to define these new technologies to include the press" (p. 59).

Nevertheless, incorporating a definition inclusive of these technologies defined as "the press" infers the process of two-way communication. Before the Internet can be defined as "part of the press," numerous questions should be addressed. Is the Internet a "common carrier not liable for content of messages and prohibitive to compromise content?" Are they broadcasters with a duty to offer some rights of access or should they be treated like the print media? Do online electronic newspapers qualify as the press? If so, does this guarantee electronic publishers immunity from government restraints?

Simply stated, it has been argued that "if an organization does not perform any constitutional function of the press, it should not qualify for constitutional designation as "the press" (Garry, 1996, p. 158). As we examine First Amendment issues relating to the media and define the restrictions of government, it is also necessary to have a clear depiction of what constitutes the press, and whether we will define the Internet as publisher or broadcaster.

CHAPTER 2 _____

The Internet: A Tool for Merchandising and Persuasion

Analyzing the Internet as a tool for merchandising and persuasion presents a number of unique perspectives that are characteristic of this evolving technology. Its ability to reach a mass audience and confront them with intimacy that contradicts traditional precepts of a mass medium is indicative of its technology and content. Therefore, issues related to privacy, morality and policy become part of a context inherent to the Internet's design and its manifestation of power. Clearly, its impact upon children is critical to the discussion of policy and the regulation of children's advertising on the Web.

AN ANALYSIS OF STRUCTURE & DESIGN

The Internet is a loose collection of computers throughout the world that share information and files. The common feature among all participants on the Internet is their willingness to use the same transmission language—Transmission Control Protocol / the Internet Protocol (TCP/IP). The result is a global collection of computers linked by telephone lines.

The Internet is a "vast central network of high-speed telephone lines designed to link and carry computer information worldwide"

(Defleur, 1996, p. 34). In addition, it is also the first mass medium that can access various forms of mass communication without experiencing government intervention. In fact, practically no one can control the manner in which information flows from one place to another. For example, an e-mail message can travel through an Internet host and its exact path is controlled neither by the sender or the recipient. This offers tremendous autonomy and freedom—and a nightmare for regulators.

The Internet was developed in the 1960's by the Defense Department to "allow military and academic researchers to conduct sensitive government probes that would survive even in the event of a nuclear disaster" (Defleur, 1996, p. 36). It was purposely designed with no central authority. The rationale was that the Internet should be designed so that no individual could own the system and that no one could kick others off the network, especially in the event of an emergency. At its beginning stages of development, primarily the government and university research departments used the Internet. No one predicted the mass appeal it would generate.

Through the Internet, transmission of information can be delivered in a spontaneous and automated basis. Therefore, normal print media and the Internet are treated differently from a legal standpoint. Internet technology has provided us all with the ability to copy and transmit information through the Internet in digitized form. Computer users now have the ability to convert copyrighted materials, visual art works texts and sound recordings into a digital form that can be displayed and transmitted using computers. The ability to take information in a variety of forms and convert it into a digital form is the main reason that the Internet is a new and different tool. It is also the reason why many laws governing copyright and other publishing matters no longer apply very well. On June 26, 1997, the Supreme Court ruled that the Internet was not like broadcast media for purposes of First Amendment protections. The result of that decision is that Internet communications are entitled to full First Amendment protection and that the Internet is free to facilitate free and open communication.

A major reason the Internet is unique is in its "increasing convergence of mass media" (Defleur, 1996, p. 40). What this means is that the Internet is often used to promote other forms of mass communication and will do so without the fear of government interference. Critics opposed to the amount of freedom flowing on the Internet are concerned that the absence of regulation is generating an environment of chaos. The volume of information available on the Internet has resulted in a voluminous amount of "cyberspace litter." And as the Internet attains commercial success, public and private institutions are debating who will have control over developing its content or technology. Critics also argue that attempting to increase its privatization would destroy its primary purpose.

Several individuals have contributed to the evolution and development of the Internet as a mass medium. Three men in particular have distinguished themselves as leaders in merchandising the Internet. Although they come from different backgrounds, and have different abilities, their common need to popularize the Internet has created a convergence in their philosophies. Each of these individuals has had a tremendous impact on the continuing development of the Internet.

Andrew Grove, Chairman of Intel

In a press conference in 1997, Andrew Grove told a panel of editors that within a few years, "Companies that don't come to grips with how the Internet works will radically alter the way businesses communicate with each other and their customers risk getting swept away" (Brennan, 1997, n.p.). The Intel Corporation, one of the leaders in this industry, can claim credit for "inventing some of the most important technologies of the modern electronics industry and bringing them successfully to the mass market" (Jackson, 1997, p. 12).

In his book, *Only the Paranoid Survive,* Grove (1996) uses his much publicized paranoia of the competition as a "tool for management" (Jackson, 1997, p. 12). He argues that companies need to be aware of the dramatic changes in the business environment and be ready to respond immediately.

Founded by Grove in 1968, Intel controls more than 80% of the market for microprocessors that run computers and is second only to Microsoft in influence in the personal computer industry. Grove helped to establish Intel as a major force behind the creation of "Silicon Valley," the site of the modern electronics industry in the San Francisco Bay area. Grove identifies the Internet as the "most powerful force facing Intel, along with the rest of the computer industry" (Jackson, 1997, p. 12). Intel has recently developed a system called MMX (Multimedia Extension) which is a new enhanced multimedia microprocessor line designed to make music sound more resonant, video images flow more smoothly, and graphic colors look richer.

Bill Gates, Chairman, Microsoft Corp.

Microsoft Chairman Bill Gates has not only revolutionized the computer software industry: he has also had a tremendous impact on establishing the Internet as a global medium. He has focused Microsoft research and development directly at the Internet and wants to build a multi-billion dollar business out of the World Wide Web. Recently, Gates came under fire by the federal government for creating a monopoly within the industry. The Microsoft Corporation was accused of creating an illegal monopoly within the software industry. James Barksdale of Netscape testified that "Microsoft's abuse of its monopoly power unless addressed through enforcement of our antitrust laws will adversely affect the course of American commerce and communications in the information age" (Goodin, 1998, n.p.).

In a hearing conducted by the United States Senate Judiciary Committee, Bill Gates of Microsoft, Michael Dell of Dell, Scott McNealy of Sun Microsystems, and James Barksdale of Netscape Communications all testified in an investigation regarding software competition and antitrust regulation. The Senate Judiciary Committee Chairman, Orrin Hatch, stated, "the hearing was not intended as a forum for criticizing or attacking any single company" (Senate Investigates, 1998, n.p.). The purpose of the investigation is to examine "how antitrust regulations should evolve to ensure competition and innovation in the computer industry" (Senate Investigates, 1998, n.p.) and to educate Congress and the public.

Antitrust laws are designed to restrain trusts, monopolies or other combinations of business and capital with a view to maintain and promote competition. One of the main areas of discussion in the hearing questioned whether Microsoft holds a monopoly for "computer operating systems, the software that controls a computer's basic task" (Senate Investigates, 1998, n.p.). Gates has repeatedly denied that Microsoft has a monopoly in the "business of developing and licensing computer operating systems" ("Senate Investigates," 1998, n.p.). The Justice Department challenged his claim that Microsoft holds 13 percent of all operating systems. They discovered that Microsoft controls 86 percent of the personal computer market. Gates defended his position by stating, "the software industry that contributed over 100 billion to the national economy last year is an open economic opportunity for any entrepreneur in America" ("Senate Investigates," 1998, n.p.).

The antitrust investigation into Microsoft was based on an allegation that Microsoft had illegally tried to force Netscape Communication to agree to a plan to divide the Internet software market. Microsoft denied these charges. As the Senate continued to examine the case against Microsoft, the focus remained on how antitrust policy could best serve consumers and the long term health of the software industry. Chairman Hatch concluded, "there is a need for an Internet commerce committee to prevent Microsoft from building its' own proprietary Internet" (Yang, 1998, n.p.).

Steve Jobs, CEO, Apple Inc.

Steve Jobs founded Apple Computer Inc. at the age of 21 in 1976 with his partner Steve Wozniak. After a messy power struggle, Jobs was forced out in 1985 only to return a decade later to revitalize the struggling company.

Apple co-pioneered the development of the personal computer by developing the Macintosh. The Macintosh became an industry standard and upset the equilibrium of International Business Machines (IBM). Macintosh, a product of Apple Inc. has had a direct impact on the first personal computers. When Macintosh was first introduced in 1984, it gave IBM a shake-up. "Macintosh computers were designed with a mouse and a set of little pictures on the screen called icons. This assisted in making the computer more user friendly to a mass audience" (Jackson, 1997, p. 277). Apple was a threat to not only IBM, but to Intel as well.

Apple became a threat to Intel because "Intel knew that the Mac's usability advantages posed a long term threat to the personal computer architecture and by extension to Intel itself" (Jackson, 1997, p. 277). However, Intel's business did not focus strictly on the personal computer. "Personal computers remained low on the list of the target marks into which the company was trying to sell its processors" (p. 202). Intel's business was based partly on its relationship with IBM. Intel's first sale of memory chips to IBM brought Intel over $1 billion dollars of revenue over five years. This helped establish an Intel processor for IBM's first personal computer. Any competition to IBM was a threat to Intel because, "Intel was still in part a prisoner of the PC industry" (p. 306). IBM was one of its biggest customers. Apple helped to revolutionize the user's role in establishing computers as a mass medium.

THE CENTER FOR MEDIA EDUCATION

Founded in 1991, the Center for Media Education (CME) is a national non-profit organization dedicated to improving the quality of the electronic media for children and to further telecommunications policy. CME was initiated to carry on the work for Action for Children's Television (ACT), which ceased operations in 1992. Their primary focus, like that of ACT, is with children. One of their first efforts, in 1992, was to spearhead a national campaign for Kids' TV. Armed with other child advocacy groups, education, and parent's groups, their efforts resulted in a 1996 decision by the FCC to require all television stations to air a minimum of three hours of educational children's programs per week. The CME has continued to promote telecommunications policies on behalf of children and has also worked with the economically disadvantaged and minorities to expand their access to new educational technologies in school and at home.

In March 1996, CME released a study, *Web of Deception: Threats to Children from On-line Marketing.* CME researched and monitored on-line developments, analyzed Websites, surveyed trade publications and special reports, and interviewed experts within the media and advertising industries. Their major concern was that advertisers would continue to develop new interactive advertising and marketing techniques as the Internet continued to become more accessible for children. And it would target the "lucrative cybertot category" (CME, 1996, n.p.). CME also stated

If the practices documented in this report go unchecked, they will sharply erode the privacy of children and their families, transform the online experience for most children into one of seductive and incessant hucksterism, and subject them to new forms of manipulation and exploitation. With the online interactive media still in their early stages of development, there is a unique opportunity to develop safeguards for ensuring that children will be treated fairly by marketers and advertisers. Although there may be hesitancy to take regulatory action regarding this new and evolving medium, adopting a "wait-and-see" attitude on the issue of marketing practices targeting children is not sensible. Without safeguards, the new forms of marketing to children online will be governed only by the marketplace" (CME, 1997, n.p.).

The new technological screening software services, e.g., Surf Watch, Cyber Patrol, Net Nanny, SafeSurf, CYBERsitter, are also not likely to adequately address the problems presented by online advertising and marketing to children. Most of these software programs were developed to protect children from sexual materials, rather than manipulative advertising and intrusive marketing practices. Even if software were created that could effectively screen out such practices, its value would be limited to those parents who could afford it, learn how to use it, and to devote the time needed to install and regularly update it.

As Congress debates regulations for the Internet, the only law affecting children and the Internet that is being addressed is the area of obscenity law. On February 8, 1996 President Clinton signed into law the Federal Communications Decency Act which banned the communication of "obscene or indecent" material via the Internet to anyone under 18 years of age. As part of the Telecommunications Act of 1996, this law received much criticism. On June 26, the Supreme Court held that the Communications Decency Act violated the First Amendment's guarantee of freedom of speech and ruled it unconstitutional and a violation of the First Amendment.

Through their investigation, the CME uncovered two kinds of threats that tracked children on-line. The first threat dealt with invasion of children's privacy. Privacy laws are one of the most discussed and confused areas of on-line law. Since the Internet is a global form of communication, should restriction lie with the sender or receiver of the message? One common argument about privacy and the Internet states, "while privacy is certainly a good thing, we don't go on-line for privacy, but to engage in new forms of community. Wrapping ourselves in too much privacy may defeat attempts to create on-line community" (Rose, 1995, p. 165).

To encourage children to read their Websites and to participate in on-line surveys, marketers have devised a way to collect data and compile individual profiles of children. Offering free gifts and opportunities to win great prizes is just one way this is accomplished. The goal of the marketer is to create an individualized personalized interactive ad that is designed to target the individual child.

As the area of privacy law and children continues to be a growing concern, the FTC recently took its first formal position on this matter. The FTC Bureau of Consumer Protection established a set of principles to help guide future decisions about how the government will watch sites aimed at minors. The set of principles is that Websites, "must disclose how they will use any personal information gathered from children and must notify parents and give parents the opportunity to control the collection or use of information about their children" (Drummond, 1996, n.p.).

The second type of threat deals with unfair and deceptive advertising. Compared to regulation imposed by the FDA and various other federal agencies, there are no guidelines enforced to limit the type of advertising shown on the Internet. Advertisers have intentionally designed Websites to capture children's attention over a period of time. Due to the lack of regulation, none of the online services such as America On-line, CompuServe, or Prodigy are subject to any restraints in this area. Children are being enticed by clicking on their favorite characters and from there are transported to specific advertising sites.

When interviewed by the CME, ad agencies admit they have hired cultural anthropologists to examine kids' culture and psychologists to study how children process information and respond to advertising. In their attempts to bring their concerns to national attention, the CME recommended the implementation of the following principles to guide the development of on-line commercial children's services:

• Personal information should not be collected from children nor should personal profiles of children be sold to third parties.

• Advertising and promotions targeted at children should be clearly labeled and separated from content.

• Children's content areas should not be directly linked to advertising sites.

• There should be no direct interaction between children and product spokes-characters.

• There should be no online micro-targeting of children, and no direct response marketing.

Children are not always aware that they are watching an advertisement. In response to the CME's set of guidelines, the FTC began to take some action because it was anxious to strengthen consumer confidence in the electronic marketplace. In another CME study, popular children's Websites were examined. The CME found certain trends and concluded the following:

• Ninety percent of Websites examined collected personally identifiable information from children.

• No site obtains verifiable parental consent before collecting the information. Only one in five sites ask children to check with their parents before releasing information.

• Forty percent of Websites used free incentives to encourage children to release personal information about themselves.

• Several sites use product spokescharacters to solicit information from children.

• One-fourth of sites send an e-mail message to children after their initial visit.

• Cookies were used by 40% of the sites.

• Websites offered no statement about information collection and use.

As a result of this study, the CME and the Consumer Federation of America requested that the FTC issue guidelines for tracking and collecting information from children on the Internet. Those guidelines are:

• All disclosure statements must be full and effective. They must include the information collected or tracked, how it is being tracked, how the information will be used, who is collecting the information, and who will have access to it.

• Parental consent needed to be obtained for the consent to be valid and the burden of consent fell on the collector to obtain valid parental consent.

• Parents should be able to correct information already collected about and from their children.

• Parents must be able to prevent the further use of their children's information after it has been collected.

The Center for Media Education also conducted a study called *Alcohol and Tobacco on the Web: New Threats to Youth* to determine the potential harmful effects that alcohol and tobacco advertising has on today's youth. Their basic findings showed that both alcohol and tobacco industries employed similar promotion techniques designed to appeal to children. Alcohol and tobacco companies offer interactive games and contests that incorporate popular icons used from popular promotions. They also provide free giveaways of branded merchandise including hip-hop clothing and drinking products. The Center for Media Education concluded the following:

• Major alcohol beverage companies are a growing commercial presence on the Web, with more than 35 brands represented.

• While regulatory constraints and fear of political backlash have kept most of the big tobacco companies from launching advertising Websites, recent developments suggest that they may be poised to move online. In the winter of 1997, the Brown & Williamson Tobacco Corporation began running Lucky Strike print ads in the San Francisco area in an effort to bring new visitors to the Website for Circuit Breaker, an online magazine that collects information on smoking habits and offers free t-shirts. Some tobacco companies have launched youth-appeal Websites in other countries, which are easily accessed in the U.S.

• Numerous other Websites and homepages are dedicated to smoking, a number of them run by commercial entities. These have helped foster an online Smoking-Is-Cool culture, which runs contrary to prevailing attitudes among most Americans about smoking and health.

• Websites promoting alcohol and tobacco employ a number of techniques. Some are an extension of the marketing and promotion efforts utilized elsewhere; others are designed to take advantage of the unique properties of the interactive online media. Many of these techniques are particularly appealing to children and youth.

• Hundred of Websites offer wine, beer, distilled spirits and tobacco products for sale on the Internet with few or no questions asked. Products purchased are delivered directly to homes. When sellers do ask if a buyer is age 21, there is no mechanism for verifying the answer.

PRIVACY AND THE COLLECTION OF PERSONAL INFORMATION

Telecommunications and computer databases have made it too easy to invade the private lives of individuals. As the Information Age reaches maturity, its tentacles seem to stretch into every aspect of our lives. It is now possible for companies to gather information about us without our knowledge. Vast amounts of personal information is being collected, sorted, and organized by both government and private entities and then used for a wide variety of purposes.

The 'Right to Privacy' is a battle cry we often hear these days as we see privacy being invaded by the onslaught of technology. However, legal scholars and the courts have had difficulty identifying the specific source of this right and in defining it scope and application. Many people believe this right emanates from the Constitution. While it may, the U.S. Supreme Court has never expressly recognized a constitutionally based right to privacy relating to the collection and use of personal information. It is therefore useful to consider that there may be no such single "right". Rather, privacy rights will take different forms depending on the type of personal information involved, how it was gathered, and what it is being used for. In each context, the right is not absolute, but must be balanced against other competing interests of the public, law enforcement, government agencies and private commercial interests. "Since privacy protections are not expressly stated in the Constitution or from comprehensive state or federal statutes, the laws developed in response to each invasion of privacy by a new technology" (Street, 1997, p. 123). These rights are generally found in the Privacy Act of 1974, the Freedom of Information Act, and the Electronic Communication Privacy Act of 1986.

Beyond the information collected by online service providers, many users of the World Wide Web are unaware that visiting various Websites or simply "surfing the Web" creates a wake of information about themselves. This personal information can easily be used and gathered for marketing and other purposes. For example, Netscape Navigator has a feature that allows the creator of a Website to customize the appearance of a Web page for someone returning to the Website after their initial visit. This is accomplished by the Web page and browser storing a file, referred to as a "cookie," on the hard disk of the user. The cookie file contains information about the user's previous access to the Website and could also be accumulated by the Website and used for its own purposes. Some browsers permit the user to refuse to accept a "cookie file storage," and some Websites will not allow access if the Web browser has been configured to refuse cookie files. However, this is not universal and most Web users do not understand that records of their activities are maintained by Websites using the disk space of the individual user.

In addition to the above, electronic mail is increasing as an efficient method of soliciting customers and selling products. Mass mailing of unsolicited e-mail containing sales promotions is referred to as "spamming." Though the FTC is currently warning "spammers" "that it will prosecute those companies that falsify return addresses in their messages" (Hot Off the Presses, 1997, p. 8), electronic junk mail is a growing problem.

Privacy advocacy groups claim that self-regulation by the industry will not safeguard personal privacy and they urge government legislation and/or regulation concerning the methods used by marketers to use the information they gather from tracking the Internet user. These advocacy groups point out that their proposals are not similar to the Communications Decency Act because they do not propose the regulation of content on the Internet but establish consumer safeguards and good companies would not be penalized for offering strong privacy protection.

On January 6, 1997, the FTC issued a report regarding *Consumer Privacy in the Online Marketplace.* (The Report can be found at the FTC's Website (www.ftc.gov) under "Conferences, Hearings, and Workshops.") The findings of the report relating to children state the U.S. law provides special protections for children. Industry groups have also imposed self-regulations to protect children. Though companies have in the past and continue to gather information about children for marketing purposes, the collection and use of this information is not subject to government regulation. The problem is in the fact that the transmission of information by a child online can easily occur without the knowledge of a parent. Information can also be more easily elicited from a child online and the parent may not even be aware that the communication occurred. The interactive nature of Websites also allows for higher levels of contact than is available over other media such as television.

Privacy groups would like to see provisions for requiring parental consent before information is gathered from children online. However, some of the difficulties in implementing this objective include:

• Deciding what ages would require parental consent.
• How to verify that the age represented by a child online is the correct age.
• How to determine whether the parent has actually consented, or whether the child pretended to be a parent.

The desire to grant parents control is generally accepted among both privacy and commercial groups. The problem is in determining what mechanism to use to achieve this result. The options are industry self-regulation, government regulation, and technological regulation. Technological regulation is the most appealing because it can be easily implemented, can reflect individual and consumer choice, can span national borders and can place a barrier between children and lawbreakers.

Several bills recently introduced by Congress deal with privacy of information concerning children. One is the Communications Policy and Consumer Empowerment Act, which would require the FTC to determine whether parents currently have the ability to exercise privacy rights regarding their children, or to determine how to provide these rights. Another recent bill, the Children's Privacy Protection and Parental Empowerment Act of 1996 would prohibit the sale of personal information and use of information about children, collected through games, contests or other means, and use of information, to contact a child except in connection with such game or contest.

According to the Center for Media Education (CME), Web advertising to children poses two kinds of threats. The first threat deals with the invasion of children's privacy through the solicitation of personal information and tracking online computer use. In this case, marketers have devised a variety of techniques to collect detailed data and to compile individual profiles on children. For example, children are offered free gifts like t-shirts or chances to win prizes such as portable CD players if they fill out an online survey about themselves. Tracking technologies make it possible to monitor every interaction between a child and an advertisement with the goal of creating personalized interactive ads designed to "micro-target" the individual child. The second threat involves the exploitation of vulnerable, young computer users through unfair and deceptive forms of advertising. Other online advertising practices have been developed which would violate long-standing safeguards protecting children in other media. But because neither proprietary online services such as America Online, CompuServe, and Prodigy, nor the World Wide Web are subject to such regulations, marketers are able to pursue children with few or no restraints. As a result, advertising and content are often interwoven into online 'infomercials' for children. Entire electronic advertising "environments" have been built to entice children to spend countless hours playing with such popular product "characters" as Tony the Tiger, Chester Cheetah and Snap! Crackle! & Pop! Interactive forms of product placement are continually being developed to encourage children to click on icons in their favorite games and play areas and immediately be transported to advertising sites.

The data gathering effort is at the heart of many children's Websites. Under the appearance of a contest ("Please fill out the form, win valuable prizes"), or as an act of fellowship ("Good citizens of the web," reads the Batman Forever site, "help Commissioner Gordon with the Gotham Census"), children are asked to fill out online forms that let advertisers know exactly who their audience is. Adults are equipped to handle these inquiries, but it is unlikely that a child, with the lure of a prize or a "free membership," will be so resistant. The questions, such as requests for age, name, address, telephone, and the number and age of siblings, are fairly invasive.

Personal data collection does not end with information given voluntarily. Web technology permits the collection of an enormous amount of data concerning the participant's online travels, tracing how he jumps from one page to another, or within a particular site, while he completes forms and makes choices. The industry term for this navigational data is the "clickstream" and even if the technology for collecting and analyzing such data is still in its childhood, there's no question that it's headed our way.

WEB OF DECEPTION: THE JOE CAMEL ADVERTISING CAMPAIGN

Through the World Wide Web, marketing to children has become a multi-billion dollar business. "Purchases made for children under 12 by parent's make-up over $14 billion dollars in revenue, teenagers another $67 billion, and together they influence $160 billion of their parents' annual spending" (Montgomery, 1996, n.p.). Unlike one-way television advertising, advertising on the Internet is interactive. Many Websites encourage children to play games and to give their opinion hoping that this will build a lasting relationship between their products and children. Their objectives are realized by a number of persuasive tools that have been tested on various audiences. Creating a cartoon character to endorse products is a time-tested tool for reaching children (i.e., Mickey Mouse, Bullwinkle, Superman, etc.).

Tobacco companies who traditionally pandered to adult audiences have re-defined their focus, and turned their attention to children.

Advertising their product with a personable cartoon figure like Joe Camel generated more interest than they could have ever imagined. Joe Camel became an icon of the children's consumer culture with teenagers and young adults embracing his message and pattern of behavior. This is a classic case of advertising creating a need in a vulnerable group of consumers such as children. Joe Camel enunciates the degree of manipulation tobacco companies will stoop to in their attempt to increase the competitive market share of their product. The Joe Camel character defines the essence of symbolic advertising that utilizes the psychology of persuasion as a tool to perpetuate a behavioral change in children.

In a study entitled, *Alcohol and Tobacco on the Web: New Threats to Youth, the CME* (1997) attempted to determine the potential harmful effects that alcohol and tobacco advertising has on today's youth. Over the years, the focus for this research was on television and print advertising. Now with the growing influence on the Internet, many previously regulated companies have no restrictions or laws regarding their advertising on the Web.

The basic findings showed that both alcohol and tobacco industries employ similar promotion techniques that are designed to appeal to children. More than 35 alcohol companies are represented on the Web. While tobacco companies are less prominent on the Web, they still manage to market to new visitors on the Web by producing an online magazine that collects information on smoking habits and by giving away free products (CME, 1998). Both alcohol and tobacco companies offer interactive games and contests, which usually incorporate popular icons, used from previous popular promotions. They also provide free giveaways of branded merchandise including hip-hop clothing and alcoholic drinking products.

The Joe Camel Advertising Campaign became a case in point. The RJ Reynolds Tobacco Company, the manufacturer of Camel cigarettes, successfully advertised and appealed to many children and adolescents under 18. Many young people were induced to either begin smoking or to continue smoking cigarettes, which resulted in significant health and safety issues.

In 1987, ads and promotions for Camel brand cigarettes had their central theme a cartoon camel called "Old Joe," "Smooth Character," or "Joe Camel." During the first three years of Joe Camel advertisements, the cigarette company's share of the under 18 cigarette market jumped from 0.5 % to 32.8 %, representing a $476 million increase in annual sales.

The FTC alleged that the purpose of the Joe Camel campaign was to reposition the Camel brand to make it attractive to younger smokers. According to the FTC complaint, the Joe Camel campaign was successful in appealing to many children and adolescents under the age of 18 and induced many of these underage consumers to smoke Camel cigarettes or increase the risk that they would do so. For many of these children and adolescents, the decision to smoke Camel cigarettes was a decision to begin smoking; for others, it was a decision to continue smoking. According to the FTC, young smokers' health was at risk because cigarettes have the potential to cause numerous diseases and other adverse health effects.

The FTC also stated that RJ Reynolds knew or should have known that the Joe Camel campaign would have a substantial appeal to children and adolescents below the age of 18 as well as to smokers over 18; or that most smokers initiate smoking and become regular smokers before the age of 18 and that by targeting "first usual brand" smokers, the Joe Camel campaign would cause many children and adolescents to smoke Camel cigarettes.

The FTC's complaint challenged the Joe Camel campaign as an unfair practice under Section 5 of the FTC Act. In order to uphold the charges before an administrative judge, the FTC needed to provide evidence to support a determination that the law had been violated. On July 30, 1996, the FTC received a letter and petition from 65 members of the U.S. House of Representatives requesting that they reopen a prior investigation of the Joe Camel campaign. In a letter dated April 9, 1997, Senator Frank R. Lautenberg and six U.S. Senators made a similar request. Though the FTC had concluded in 1994 there was insufficient evidence to issue a complaint, the petition from the Members of Congress requested that they reexamine that decision.

On May 28, 1997, the FTC charged the R.J. Reynolds Tobacco Company with violating federal law and promoting an addictive and dangerous product to children and adolescents under the age of 18 through a campaign that was attractive to those too young to purchase cigarettes legally. The FTC also said that the percentage of kids who smoked Camels became larger than the percentage of adults who smoked Camels.

Following the administrative trial, the FTC sought an order to prohibit R.J. Reynolds from advertising its Camel brand cigarettes to children through the use of images or themes relating or referring to Old Joe, Smooth Character or Joe Camel. The cigarette manufacturer would have to conduct a public education campaign discouraging youth from smoking. In addition, the company would make available for inspection competent and reliable data concerning sales of cigarettes to anyone under the age of 18. The FTC could also order relief, such as corrective advertising or other affirmative disclosures, after the trial on the case had concluded. On July 10, 1997, R.J. Reynolds Tobacco Company announced that its 23-year old Joe Camel advertising campaign would be discontinued.

Although the FTC had been relatively successful in dealing with the Joe Camel campaign, alcohol and tobacco companies continue to use a variety of marketing techniques that capitalize on the medium's strong and unique attraction for young people. These campaigns are being launched at a time when drinking and smoking among youth are at alarmingly high levels. Underage drinking and smoking is already a major public health problem in the U.S. In addition, alcohol is a factor in all leading causes of death for young people between the ages of 15 to 24. While smoking among adults is declining, smoking among youth is on the rise. Advertising and marketing play a major role in influencing the drinking and smoking behavior of youth.

Alcohol companies promote "bridge drinks," sweet concoctions that disguise the taste of alcohol to appeal to novice drinkers. They also invent brand spokes characters to match bios of typical college kids. Tobacco companies invite kids to partake in chat rooms like Smokey's Café where they find photos of celebrities smoking, feature pro-smoking articles, and see lists of cigarette and cigar vendors. Vendors offer discounts in exchange for filling out market surveys, which collect personal data. Although there are no established guidelines for marketing alcohol and tobacco products on the Internet, they have violated existing laws towards marketing their products to minors. Both alcohol and tobacco companies sell their products on the Internet without verifying the age requirements of their consumers. The CME has argued that

> the Cigarette Act which has kept advertising of cigarettes off radio and television applies to any medium of electronic communication subject to the jurisdiction of the FCC, should also apply to the Internet. (CME, 1997)

Although the restrictions appear similar, the Internet is unlike any other medium of electronic communication. The owner of the wire is a common carrier. According to Wallace, "Internet access providers are free to pick and choose the speech that may reach the Internet, by implication they may join together to determine that certain categories of speech, though legal, will never see the light of day" (Wallace & Mangan, 1996, p. 257). The same persuasions can be made for advertising. If Diet Coke, which contains saccharin, an artificial preservative was thought to be addicting to children, would we also regulate advertising because of the possible negative impacts the product could have?

According to findings that appeared in the April 1996 issue of the Journal of Marketing, minors are three times more responsive to cigarette advertisements than adults. The findings buttress the FDA's interest in restricting tobacco advertising deemed accessible to minors (Noah, 1996, p. 37).

The alcoholic beverage industries have self-regulatory guidelines that prohibit targeting underage youth. However, these rules appear to have little impact on the Web marketing of many companies. Screening software programs and blocking technologies such as Net Nanny and Cyber Patrol can be somewhat helpful; however, these technologies will not adequately protect children and youth from online marketing of alcohol and tobacco. The seamless interweaving of content and advertising, the ever-changing nature of Web content itself, and the use of surreptitious techniques like those employed in the Lucky Strike promotion, are likely to hinder efforts to effectively screen out these forms of marketing. Screening devices do little to protect underage youth in colleges, where binge drinking is a major public health problem. The alcohol industries can promise not to promote their products on college campuses but they have a direct line into the dorm of nearly every student.

CASHING IN ON CHILDREN: THE CHILD MARKET

The World Wide Web was created as a simple system to retrieve information on the Internet; as a marketing device, the Web is now the hot new tool of the times. With the click of a mouse, any 'home page' can present text, sound and video and also steer the user to other sites a world away. The Internet is more powerful than any other electronic medium previously seen. It has the ability to appeal directly to children, with colorful, fun-filled "playrooms," where the distinction between fact and fiction, between programming and advertising, is all but obscured. As the technology continues to mature and become more interactive, marketers can track online activities, generate profiles of someone's tastes and make personalized appeals to children that are difficult to resist.

The commercial implications of kids online have not been lost on corporate America. Advertising designed to attract children is no small matter. On television alone, it is approaching $800 million in annual ad revenue for children's programming. Although online advertising hasn't approached those numbers yet, there is a great potential for significant online advertising revenues. And the number of children online is growing rapidly. According to Jupiter Communications, publisher of the *Digital Kids Report,* nearly 3.7 million children under the age of 18 have Web access and that figure is rapidly growing. Of those who currently have Web access, nearly a million use it, and the industry has picked up on the trend. Most of the commercial online services have established special areas aimed at children, e.g. the "Kids Only" section of America Online, "Just Kids" on Prodigy, and a child-friendly "Wow"!" on CompuServe. The services view this as an important growth area for their highly competitive operations. Even more competition looms as Disney, Nickelodeon, and Scholastic, among others, plan to launch stand-alone systems targeting the family market.

The major online services have not overlooked the potential for increased advertising revenues from kids. The Nickelodeon site, little more than an advertising campaign, is leading the way in selling online space for third-party ads directed at children. Only a mouse-click on the icon of a Band-Aid separates a child from its advertisers. In online children's programming, advertisers are gaining increased access to children.

In one of the more popular Websites aimed at children, there is the greeting, "Welcome aboard, cybernauts! We're SNAP! CRACKLE! POP!" says the Kellogg Clubhouse. In exchange for an e-mail address, you are invited into the clubhouse and can "Chill with Crackle! "Party with Pop!, or "Slide with Snap!" In addition, there are other pleasures, nearly all of which are tied to various Kellogg cereals. A Kellogg's screensaver is available for downloading color photos of the Kellogg

NASCAR racing team. A graphical history of souvenir items is offered on Kellogg cereal boxes going back to 1933. And there are similar histories of Tony the Tiger, Toucan Sam, Dig'em, Coco, and other characters, along with brand-related comic strips, coloring books, and interactive games.

Snap, Crackle, and Pop are not alone on this new digital frontier. Many other companies are greeting kids online, with everyone from Frito Lay's Chester Cheetah to Disney's Pocahontas, from GI Joe to Batman. There are also gathering places for children all over the Web, including sites maintained by Fox Broadcasting, Warner Brothers, Toys 'R' Us, Time-Warner, Nintendo, and Sega. It is estimated that one-third of the 15 million current Websites are corporate cyber-homes, and the number is growing rapidly.

In her study of preadolescent children's attitudes toward television commercials, Clara Ferguson (1975) writes,

> The child market has three important facets. First, preadolescent children represent a substantial and significant consumer market for many product categories. Second, they are an influential force in the purchase of products directly consumable as well as those used by the entire family. Third, they represent a future adult consumer market whose attitudes towards products advertised and toward television commercials are in the process of formation" (Ferguson, 1975, p. 4–5).

James McNeal, in his study, *Children as Consumers,* concluded, "Children play an active consumer role, attributable to such factors as industrialization, urbanization, increased family income, more leisure time, and more permissive child-training" (p. 68). In a later study, McNeal (1969) noted, "that the child market is sizable, that it has the desire and ability to buy, and that it has some degree of understanding of money and the purchase process" (p. 15).

The child market, therefore not only plays an active consumer role but is also an influential agent in the purchase decision for many products. Findings from research by Scott Ward and Daniel Wackman (1971),

> indicate that the strongest purchase-influence attempts by children are for relevant food products and durables, such as games, toys, clothing, bicycles, and record albums. In addition, children attempt to

influence, although to a lesser degree, the purchase of notions, toiletries, automobiles, gasoline brands, laundry soap, and household cleansers — products used by all family members" (Ferguson, 1975, pp. 4–5).

According to Ward (1972),

television advertising is .... one input in developmental processes by which young people acquire knowledge, attitudes, and skills relating to consumer behavior. Among young people such consumer behavior can be relatively immediate, such as the expenditure of allowance, earnings, etc. In other cases, the behavior may involve attempts to influence the purchases of others, such as parents and friends. (p 63)

With children as such an key force in the market, it is no wonder that advertisers have gone to great lengths to capture their attention and loyalty.

CHAPTER 3

Advertising: Children as Products
of a Consumer Culture

Advertising has been around for at least four thousand years, but its early use and applications were limited to messages scratched on walls, placed on signs and heralded by criers. Archeologists have uncovered many such "signs," notably in the ruins of ancient Rome and Pompeii. And in the Middle Ages, the use of so-called town criers developed. The criers were citizens who read public notices aloud and were also employed by merchants to shout the praises of their wares. In the 15th century the invention of movable type was considered the most significant technological development of the time. This led eventually to the printing of newspapers, which contained what might be considered as the first "modern" advertisements. *Harper's Weekly* observed in 1897 that "Advertisements are now part of the humanities, a true mirror of life, a sort of fossil history from which the future chronicler, if all other historical monuments were to be listed, might fully and graphically rewrite the history of our time" (cited in "Printers' Ink," 1897, p. 42).

In the early stages of American advertising, direct advertising was most effective because the nation lacked transcontinental transportation distribution and communications systems. Late in the 19th century, many American firms began to market packaged goods under brand names. Previously, such everyday products as sugar, soap, rice and molasses were sold in neighborhood stores from large bulk containers, and as a result, consumers were seldom aware of, or influenced by, brand names. Shortly after the turn of the twentieth century, Americans began to be aware of such brand names as Coca-Cola and Wrigley.

From its inception, the advertising industry has relied on creative endeavors to sell goods and services. However, by the mid-twentieth century mere creativity was no longer enough. What advertisers were looking for were more sophisticated techniques that would persuade people to buy more, so that the wheels of our mass-production, mass-consumption economy would keep turning. To develop these techniques, the advertising industry turned to consumer research to provide insights into the personalities and sub-conscious desires of the consuming public.

After World War I, advertising developed into a business so big that it became almost a trademark of America itself in the eyes of the world. The increased use of electricity led to the illuminated outdoor poster, photoengraving and other modern printing inventions, and the advent of radio in the 1920's stimulated a whole new technique of selling by voice. The most significant development after World War II was television, a medium that forced the advertising industry to better its techniques of selling by the use of visual devices as well as by voice, and gradually to rely more and more on visual images to sell their products.

According to Vance Packard (1971), who began writing about this research with alarm in the 1950s, the advertising industry started tailoring its ads to meet the needs of the id, that part of the mind that generates our most basic urges and impulses (Packard, 1971, p. 9).

Concern over the effects of advertising on children can be traced back to at least 1961 when the National Association of Broadcasters adopted guidelines regulating toy advertising on television. Today, the principle of children as a special audience needing protection has been widely accepted by both industry and government policy makers. This largely came about because of the efforts of consumer groups who accumulated a body of research on the effects of advertising on children. When television became available to the public, it was understood that the medium would be developed as a profit-making enterprise controlled by private interests whose revenues would come from advertising.

The quest to learn what motivates consumer-buying habits has seen a growing number of companies turning to psychological research on advertising. Targeting children means using data obtained when a child searches the Internet to develop advertising techniques that will stimulate a child to buy a particular product.

EFFECTS OF ADVERTISING ON CHILDREN

Research on the effects of advertising on children's behavior is not new. In the early 1930's, there was an effort to assess the effects of motion pictures on children.

Florence Brumbaugh (1954) was one of the first researchers to study the effects of television advertising on children. Her studies revealed that, "Children had excellent recall of products advertised on television, most of which were not for children's consumption, and the apparent realism of the message and the method of presentation determined children's opinions of commercials" (in Ferguson, 1975, p. 14). Brumbaugh also concluded that,

> the degree to which televised advertising is conditioning children is difficult to determine, since the same articles are usually advertised on radio and in newspapers and magazines. It is unlikely that they will remember or know which of the media influence them, or whether their attitudes were changed because of television (p. 14).

In the mid 1950's, the criminal theme content of comic books and television and its effects on children was investigated. Since television came of age as a mass medium in the early 1950's, there has been a continuing interest in the effects of television on children based on the content of television programs. Prior research on the effects of television advertising was sparse.

In 1964, James McNeal conducted a study entitled *Children as Consumers*. In this study, he stated,

> All of the children on this study reported watching television, and, with the exception of two five-year-olds, all indicated a keen awareness of TV advertisements. There was increasing dislike and mistrust of TV ads as the children increased in age. Half of the five-and seven-year-olds and over three-fourth of the nine-year-olds reported negative feelings toward television commercials. They believed that the ads are, in general, "untruthful," "annoying," "silly," "repetitious," and take too much time from the program in progress" (Ferguson, 1975, p. 21).

McNeal's study addresses issues that are also of concern to the advertising industry.

Erica Gruen (1995), Senior Vice President of Saatchi and Saatchi says,

> Kids are extremely vulnerable, and perceive themselves to be. They're tiny, they're small in relation to the adult world, and they feel themselves vulnerable, physically, mentally, and emotionally. So what does going online do? Online to kids represents the attainment of power to kids (Gruen, 1995, p. 3).

Gruen's comments also seem to suggest another kind of power, where marketers can connect directly to children, bypassing traditional parental and structural intermediaries and develop a new kind of commercial relationship with children. In addition, Gruen points out,

> Communication via the computer may easily one day rival the telephone. There are none of the traditional barriers that protect children from advertising abuse on television. No limits exist currently on the number or length of ads on the Web and online services. There is no prohibition against making a pitch directly to children. The World Wide Web is a wide-open field for companies to engage children with their goods and services and to develop brand loyalty at an early age (Gruen, 1995, p. 3).

What Gruen articulates reinforces Florence Brumbaugh's premise of the excellent recall children have for products advertised on television which are not meant for their consumption.

On the other hand, many of the products that are aimed at them are not necessarily good for them. Manufacturers of food products have a particular interest in creating Web domains that are captivating and fun for children. Erica Gruen says that developing brand loyalty and a brand environment for food products provides "an unparalleled opportunity to get kids actively involved with brands" (Gruen, 1995, p. 3).

As a policy issue, the concern for children as targets of a consumer culture, especially on television has been a subject of increased concern and debate over the past twenty years. Criticism of food advertising has been directed at the quality and range of food products advertised and at the methods used to present these foods in commercials.

The majority of commercials on television that are aimed at children are for food products and services. The FTC has been mostly concerned about the high sugar content in advertised foods. Between-meal consumption of such foods, especially when the candy or snack is sticky and can be sucked or chewed over time, is said to promote tooth decay and contribute to other health problems, such as obesity. In addition, such foods provide little nutritional value in proportion to the calories consumed. There has been concern that the foods most heavily advertised to children represent a limited range of the foods that are available for consumption. They often consist mostly of ready-to-eat cereals, candies, and other sugared snacks.

Critics contend that foods are not promoted to children on the basis of their nutritional value and food commercials neither provide nutritional information nor associate the foods being advertised with principles of good nutrition and health. Instead, advertised foods are related to attributes that are irrelevant to their inherent food value, including sweet taste or flavors, fun, adventure, hero figures and other likeable characters, and premium offers. Advertised foods are described mostly in terms of their taste, texture, and ingredients (like "sugar crunchy", or "fruit chew middle"). Sweetness or sugared taste is identified as a desirable characteristic of foods. Furthermore, the impression is given that eating such products is fully consistent with good health by showing happy, healthy children enjoying these products in the commercials.

According to Atkin and Gibson (1978), children have been shown to accept or believe many of the product claims made about advertised foods. They have also been shown to draw inferences beyond the explicit content, including mistaken inferences about what is safely edible and about the personal qualities of product presenters and characters.

A 1992 study by the Center for Science in the Public Interest found that "nine out of ten food ads on Saturday morning TV were for candy bars, sugary cereals, salty chips, or other nutritionally flawed foods" (Jacobson, 1995, p. 62). According to an FTC report looking at the effect of advertised food products on children, the types of foods advertised during Saturday morning cartoons were reviewed. Of the food advertising aimed at children, Dr. Jean Meyer of the FTC said,

> If you placed foods in decreasing order of nutritional usefulness, you would have something like this:

Group 1: Fruits and vegetables, milk, fish, eggs, meat and cheese.
Group 2: Bread, potatoes, macaroni products, some of the better breakfast cereals, soups.
Group 3: Sugarcoated breakfast cereals, most 'snack foods', cake mixes.
Group 4: Candy and soft drinks.
"It is fairly obvious to any habitual television viewer that national advertising expenditures are in reverse order to nutritional usefulness" (FTC, 1978, p. 172).

Meyer further observed that the reason for this is that foods produced in Group 1 are generally not branded and are produced by numerous autonomous farmers without advertising budgets. Foods in groups 3 and 4 are produced by only a handful of large multinational corporations with a strong brand name and with large advertising budgets. Children view commercials for sugared food products with empty calories on an almost constant basis. This advertising portrays eating these sugared foods as the "normal, pervasively accepted thing to do, either at breakfast or between meals" (p. 165). Furthermore, the advertising suggests that eating sugared foods is perfectly consistent with the concept of a healthy and balanced diet.

Advertisers are able to sell the idea that sugared foods are nutritionally valuable through a number of means. Products are often referred to as being "enriched" or "fortified" by essential vitamins. Further, sugared cereals are often sold along with the disclaimer that they should be part of a nutritious breakfast. (This breakfast typically includes cereal, milk, orange juice, toast, and fruit.) However, the message that children receive is that eating the cereal alone will provide a sufficiently healthy breakfast. A study by Atkin and Gibson (1978) examined children's understanding of this balanced breakfast concept. In the study, 4-to-7 year-old children were shown a cereal ad containing the balanced breakfast disclaimer. When asked about the commercial,

"two-thirds of the children could remember none of the foods depicted with the cereal, two thirds of the children didn't understand the meaning of the term balanced breakfast, and two thirds of the preschool subgroup thought that the cereal alone would be sufficient in providing the balanced breakfast" (Atkin, C. & Gibson, W., 1978, p. 67).

Another technique used by advertisers to sell sugared foods as nutritional is to form a close identification between a person, or more likely a cartoon character, and the food. According to Atkin and Gibson (1978), children find these cartoon characters (e.g., Fred Flintstone and Barney Rubble) to be credible and knowledgeable sources of nutritional information. (Children who are heavy TV viewers are more likely to attribute credibility to these animated characters than light viewers.)

According to Erica Gruen (1995), brand environments created by advertisers on the Internet also beckon children to "come and play." Further, children who visit a site such as Kids-Com can experience a "brand environment: and earn "Kids-Kash" by answering mind-numbing questions about various products featured elsewhere on Kids-Com. This process leads in turn to the "Loot Locker," where virtual cash can be redeemed and used to purchase the very same products. Nabisco Neighborhood, Oscar Mayer Cyber Cinema, and Colgate Kid's World are other brand environments that lure children to come and play.

These advertising sites are not used to provide nutritional information but solely to build brand loyalty in children. Scammon and Christopher (in Young, 1990) reviewed the literature on the impact of advertising sugared foods to children as nutritious and concluded that "exposure to commercials for sugared products led to greater consumption of sugared products, greater preference for sugared foods, including foods that were not advertised, and lower nutritional knowledge" (p. 133). Further, Atkin, Reeves, and Gibson (in Young, 1990) studied a group of 5-to 12-year olds and concluded that "heavy viewers of food ads on television were twice as likely as viewers to say that sugared cereals and candies (sweets) were highly nutritious" (p. 133).

THE CONTENT OF CHILDREN'S ADVERTISING

Online advertisers are not subject to the same regulations that television advertisers must adhere to. Therefore, online advertising directed at children warrants more attention. Advertisers have cleverly disguised marketing devices that can find a hiding place in a child's electronic toy chest. They have colorful online "playmates" whose goal is to sell products and to collect a child's personal data. This opens the way to exploit a child's curiosity, needs, fears, and expectations. And parents have not been properly cautioned about the way all this works.

Due to the rapid advances in the new media, there is a temptation to stand back and "see what happens" as the technology grows. However, in the area of children's programming, the potential for abuse in the form of deceptive and invasive practices, is simply too great to adopt a wait-and-see attitude.

Corporate Websites are very good at "manipulating" the consumer and it is difficult to compete with them. Marketers are continually finding new, seductive ways to reach out to children and collect information about those children that will make their sites even more irresistible in the future. Marc Rotenberg (in Center for Media Education, 1997), director of the Electronic Privacy Information Center, offers a sketch of what this new information environment might look like. He says,

> Instead of doing a commercial that's roughly targeted to boys five to seven, now you're targeting a particular boy, who has a particular interest in a particular program, who lives in a house, whose parents have a certain income. And at that level of targeting, I think the opportunity for manipulation becomes much greater, really almost overwhelming for parents who are trying to control the upbringing of their kids. Because we've never really existed before in an information environment where the TV could reach out to your child and say, "Bob, wouldn't you like to have this new action figure, just like in the movie you saw last week?" Little Bob, needless to say, will be flattered and intrigued by this new 'TV that talks back,' a device that magically remembers his last visit and tailors the next one to correspond to his special interests. Its exciting, this new, personalized, interactive media, but it's more than a little unfortunate. Bob and millions of children like him will be transformed. They won't simply be children anymore, but something more valuable to the corporations investing vast sums to develop the World Wide Web, they'll be customers (p. 6).

According to Erica Gruen, (in Center for Media Education, 1997), "marketers have to be in this playground. So it's important to create a space for kids only that's fun, exciting, and private, where kids can feel that they are, indeed, in charge" (p. 6). At a conference sponsored by Jupiter Communications she also said, "This is a medium for advertisers that is unprecedented. There is nothing else that exists like it for advertisers to build relationships with kids and there's probably no other product or service that we can think of that is like it in terms of capturing kids' interest" (p. 7). She continued,

The Kid Connection division of Saatchi and Saatchi, believes in marketing to kids from the inside out. Saatchi has sent a team of anthropologists into the homes of children to observe their online behavior.
They sort of make themselves invisible after a very short time and
were able to really watch kids at what they did. Saatchi also called in
psychologists who conducted one-on-one sessions with a sample
group of children to try to get other hidden motivators that weren't so
obvious in the observation. The objective of this research was to find
out why kids take a strong ownership to the new technology (p. 7).

The Internet is offering something whose vast preponderance is
commercially driven. Snack food giant Frito-Lay's Website offers
remarkably extensive information on the history of Fritos, Ruffles,
Tostitos, and the like. The site includes interactive cartoons for children such as dream analysis by "the world famous Freud/Jungian ana-
lyst Dr. Isac Duseldbaum," The site is complete with sound clips of
the psychiatrist's silly pronouncements, and a build-your-own "dream
date" construction kit. For parents there are the "Dream Vacations"
section, which has links to airlines, car rental agencies, tour providers,
and hotel chains. But the idea is the same—excite the viewer's interest, deliver some content, and then finish the transaction with a plug.
Duracell has a similar approach. Its site is nothing more than an interactive ad. It offers puzzles that feature toys used in past Duracell commercials and a chance to become an honorary member of the company's TV spokes-family.

When it comes to safeguarding America's children from the
potentially harmful effects of advertising, the government and the
American public are faced with many political, social and ethical
questions. There is no question that it is important to protect
America's future, its children. How can the government protect the
physical and emotional development of our children while also safeguarding their Constitutional rights? And how does Congress protect
children without infringing on the rights of American adults? These
issues are raised within the context of children's advertising, and
demand serious scrutiny.

Historically, attempts to create consumer behavior in children were
accomplished by offering premiums through a corporate sponsor that a
child could acquire. For example, the early television program "Captain

Midnight" offered children a secret decoder ring and an invisible ink pen that they could use to interact with the program. The Internet however can offer children immediate gratification by creating a conditioning environment of interactive adaptive behavior. This leads to the question of how children adapt to the use of the Internet as a technology of inquiry and as a tool for searching the Web.

In the *Journal of Consumer Research,* a study was conducted to determine age differences in information search behaviors. The basic question was "How adaptive are young children as decision makers?" The findings indicated that younger children tend to use fewer dimensions to compare and evaluate brands. Not surprisingly, children also appear to use simple choice mechanisms rather than compensatory choice strategies and tend to rely on the dominant perceptual features of products in gathering information and making choices.

For this investigation, children's search behaviors were examined within the context of a game called "House of Prizes" that involved making a choice between two "houses" containing prizes hidden behind "curtains." Children were allowed to search behind the curtains to uncover the prizes before making their choices. The study included 63 children; 33 were six to seven years of age, and 33 were four to five.

The game was structured to be engaging. Children were involved in making real choices with real consequences. Manipulations of search benefits and costs were also designed to provide an incentive for children to carefully consider their search activities. It was found that the six- to seven- year-olds modified their search behavior more in line with an appropriate cost-benefit trade-off than the four- to five- year- olds. For the older children, the least information was gathered for the least favorable cost-benefit profile and the most information was gathered for the most favorable cost-benefit profile.

In other words, sometime during the preschool years, children learn how to use the information search strategy extensively in different situations. Prior to this development children have limited ability to adjust their search strategies to particular situations. Therefore, when four to five-year-olds watch advertisements, what they see is what they believe until they reach the point where they are able to adjust their information search strategy. And since today's kids are either spending money on their own, making purchases with parental guidance or participating in family purchase decisions, the way they respond to advertising has real economic consequences.

Kids' preferences and needs also account for some big-ticket items. Joan Chiaramonte (1996), the Roper Vice-President who directs Roper's *Annual Youth Report,* commented that surveys indicate that a majority of parents consider their children one of the important reasons to buy a computer. While computers in households with kids have become fairly common, personal ownership is on the rise for 7% of 6- to 7-year- olds, 99% of preteens and 25% of teens. Seventy-seven per-cent of kids with computers at home use game software, while 57% have word processing, 45% educational programs, and 42% graphics packages.

ADVERTISING AND PIAGET'S THEORY

Over the past fifty years, developmental psychologists have worked on a theory of cognitive development, based primarily on the research of the Swiss psychologist, Jean Piaget. Our understanding of how a child's mind works from infancy until adolescence has been strongly influenced by his theories, which involve the way knowledge, understanding, and perceptions of the world grow in a child, and how the capacities of children at different ages affect their ability to process various types of information. Although there are strong qualifications to Piaget's stages, it nevertheless is very helpful in understanding how advertising can take advantage of children and their still-developing cognitive abilities.

Research on advertising to children has relied on Piaget's theories to explain how children react or respond to advertising at different stages of their development. Scott Ward (1972) was an early writer to study a specific concept from Piaget in regards to advertising. He observed that "young children's reactions to television advertising reflect stages in cognitive development" (p. 28). Critics of children's advertising have also relied upon Piaget's theories of cognitive devel-opment in children to support their contentions that much advertising to children is unfair and exploitative. This research has not gone unno-ticed. In fact, the FTC has adopted Piaget's theory as a theoretical basis for implementing its regulations.

According to Piaget, children become more competent as they grow. The development of this competency consists of four major stages: (1) sensorimotor— from birth to 2 years; (2) pre-operational—

from 2 years to 7 years; (3) concrete operational—from 7 years to 11 years; and (4) formal operational (abstract thinking)— 11 years and up. Piaget also argued that a child's cognitive performance depended more on the stage of development he was in than on the specific task being performed. Piaget (1972) further concludes that although experience supports and boosts the stage in the development process, it does not determine the child's performance or actions. He states, "We use the term stage where the series of actions is constant, independently of such speeding up or slowing down as may modify the middle range of chronological age in terms of acquired experience and social environment" (p. 17).

This view of children's behavior as being "stage dependent" was rapidly accepted by those interested in explaining the influence of television advertising. It was an already defined method of theory that conveniently predicted what children are able to do within a given stage. Since these stages were considered to have an approximate relationship with age, children were categorized in that way. A categorization of children in the seven or eight year old age range was considered to be "pre-operational". This meant that children had a limited ability to abstract and transform stimulus events around them. No amount of learning, according to Piaget, could change these basic characteristics, until the child moved onto another stage. Stimulus events included advertising to which the child was exposed.

According to John Flavel (1977), a researcher of Jean Piaget, "his model of the human cognitive system stresses the constant interaction or collaboration of the internal-cognitive with the external-environmental in the construction and employment of knowledge" (p. 8). Piaget believed that much learning originates from inside the child. An understanding of this may lead to an awareness of how a child perceives advertising. He further states,

> Until children construct a certain level of logic from within themselves, based on the experiential process, they can only base their judgement only on what they can see. According to Piaget, the process of children's construction of knowledge, is the process of moving from one level of being "wrong" to another, rather than simply accumulating more and more knowledge quantitatively (Ewing, 1996, p. 262).

Using this theory, critics viewed the advertiser as a seducer of children, playing on their innocence and creating a desire within them to want what is being advertised. Young children, without the benefit of the experiential process, can only base their judgments on what they see, and are therefore unable to make logical inferences about the advertising to which they are exposed. The business of advertising is about persuading people to buy their products. The naivete or innocence of children and their trusting nature make children more vulnerable to advertising. Young children can be easily exploited, and they are not capable of protecting themselves. Conceptions based on Piaget elicit considerable reactions opposed to child advertising that is seen as unfair.

Many theorists have explored the concept of stage development and Piaget's theories have been generally accepted. Most theorists agree with the notion of cognitive structure, the stages of development, and developmental growth. According to Wackman and Ward (1976), "The theory is useful in guiding policy decisions concerning what are and what are not appropriate marketing stimuli for children" (p. 513). A number of papers have also reviewed the concept of stage development (Ward & Wackman 1974; Ward, Wackman, & Wartella, 1975; Wartella & Ettema, 1974). Though some controversy surrounding Piaget's theory was noted, these developmental theorists generally accepted his ideas. Most developmental theorists agree with the notion of cognitive structure, the stages of development, and developmental growth. However, there is also a view that language by itself is an inappropriate method for assessing information-processing activities in young children.

Nisbett and Wilson (1977) suggest,

> When people are asked to report how a particular stimulus influenced a particular response, they do so not by consulting a memory of the mediating process, but by applying or generating causal theories about the effect of that type of stimulus on that type of response (p. 84).

It is therefore possible that older children are more sophisticated in their understanding of causal explanations that have little to do with actual information-processing events.

Evidence of strong demand characterizes children's use of language with adults has also been noted, as well as sensitivity to subtle changes in the choice of words used. Older children also exhibit an entirely different system of response. Marion Blank (1975), a noted theorist states,

> Just as the child's linguistic structure differs from that of the adult, so too may his use of language differ from the adult. As a result, he may appear not to use his language (e.g., he may not be able to relate the 'purpose' of a television commercial), when in fact the difficulty may be the adult's failure to recognize the rules of the child's verbal code (p. 46).

Further discussion of this topic is noted by Gelman (1978), who observed, "I hold that recent work supports the view that the preschooler possesses some cognitive capabilities that might be less complex than, or even different from, those of the older child, but which are nevertheless very real" (p. 297). Wartella (1981) also points out that children of a certain cognitive stage are seen as unable to perform mental operations more characteristic of another, later stage.

The explanatory concepts of Piaget's theories of stage development in children have been used to support the belief that children's advertising is unfair. While other theorists support the notion that "cognitive development is not an all-or-none process" (Gelman, 1978, p. 297). Piaget's theories remain the basis for the interest that some groups have in regulating advertising to children.

LICENSED PRODUCT MERCHANDISING AND THE WEB

Most of us are oblivious to the phenomenon of licensing, but at one time or another we have all embraced this practice by purchasing or accepting as a gift an item manufactured under license. Industry observers credit the Ideal Toy Company, for example, with the first mass-marketed licensed item, the Teddy Bear, supposedly named after and licensed by Theodore Roosevelt. The concept of product merchandising has made companies like Walt Disney into a giant character licensor. Who can forget the coonskin cap craze theme of Davy Crockett, which sold over $100 million worth of fake coonskin caps to American boys? Though Davy Crockett was not a long-term licensing phenomenon, other characters have exhibited a lengthier license merchandising life span. Mickey Mouse, Buck Rogers, and the Lone Ranger have consistently proven their merchandising clout when themed to toys and apparel. The most successful licensed product ever is the Barbie doll. The doll and its innumerable accessories has produced over $800 million in retail sales since 1958.

One of the largest agencies specializing in licensing is the Licensing Corporation of America. The company, a subsidiary of Time Warner Communications, serves as the licensing representative for a diversified clientele. LCA's line-up of clients include cartoon characters such as Bugs Bunny, motion picture characters such as Superman, sports entities such as baseball and hockey clubs, as well as to individual actors and athletes. LCA manages all aspects of the licensing business, including promotion, quality control, packaging design, auditing procedures, and royalty rates. They also publish an industry newsletter that reports on developments in the field.

In essence, the Internet has become the ultimate mass marketer. With its inherently interactive design, the Web offers a child ease of access and selection. So often, marketers huckstering their products and wares give spokes-characters a legitimate status. To many critics the ultimate insult is the merchandising of the brand spokes-character as a licensed toy for sale to children. It is a constant reminder to both parents and children of the communication-power of the Internet. For example, alcohol companies promote "bridge drinks", sweet concoctions that disguise the taste of alcohol to appeal to novice drinkers. They also invent brand spokes-characters to match the biography of typical college kids. Tobacco companies invite kids to partake in chat rooms like Smokey's Café, where they find photos of celebrities smoking, read pro-smoking articles, and see lists of cigarette and cigar vendors. Discounts are offered in exchange for filling out market surveys that collect personal data. Both alcohol and tobacco companies sell their products on the Internet without verifying the ages of their consumers. It has been argued that since the Cigarette Act has kept advertising of cigarettes off radio and television, it should apply to any medium of electronic communication subject to the jurisdiction of the FCC as well as the Internet. The Internet is unlike any other medium of electronic communication. The owner of the wire is a common carrier. According to Wallace and Mangan (1996), "Internet access providers are free to pick and chose the speech that may reach the Internet, by implication they may join together to determine that certain categories of speech, though legal, will never see the light of day" (p. 257). The same arguments can be made for advertising.

In addition to an increase in their purchasing involvement of children, there's another aspect of modern childhood that marketers find very significant. It's the tendency of kids today to desire brand names at an early age, which turns into brand loyalty in the long run. Toper Taylor (1995), senior vice-president and head of U.S. operations for Nelvana, a studio that specializes in children's animation, has observed that children have an attraction to any kind of licensed product as early as age 3. He also states that by 7 they are rushing to be the first in line to buy a specific toy.

Chapter 4

The Internet: A Tool for Enfranchisement?

The Internet is a system of computer networks. However, it is also a forum for human interaction supporting a new and unique culture. Recently it has also become a medium for popular commercial enterprise. With so many different types of publics, there is such a large diversity of information quality and quantity on the Internet, and there is no ruling body that determines what gets on it. Anyone who understands and has access to the necessary technology can put practically anything on it. This provides a wonderful means for free and open communication between people worldwide. It also makes quality control impossible.

Many writers and theorists since McLuhan have discussed the sociological implications of electronic culture, as well as its economic and political underpinnings. Relatively few have taken up McLuhan's concern with the "aesthetics" of such a culture. By this he means its sensory, affective and libidinal dimensions, the question of what it will look, sound, and feel like, and what desires will be aroused and propagated within it. In essence, how will these innovations alter consciousness itself?

We can see various effects of the Internet on our culture. It permeates all aspects of our lives, including our language, community, and our self-perception. We must re-establish ourselves to the new people we communicate with. This is because there is no inherent attribute that we project, either through attitude or nuance that is communicated before the interaction begins. In the projection of our persona across the network we are given a chance to virtually change who we are. Since there are no preconceived notions of who a person is in a virtual space, one is released from the expectation where a person tends to act as he or she is expected to. Articles have been written on the transformation of a person as well as on the potentially addictive qualities of such interactions and changes.

According to McLuhan, all media are extensions of ourselves. New technologies literally change "the ratios of our senses," as they alter the experiential structures of space and time. McLuhan prophesied that there would be radical cultural dislocations as human culture is transformed from one that is predominantly local, linear, and print-based, into one that is polyphonic, electronic, global, and dominated by multimedia. What once appeared as visionary and controversial has now become generally accepted to the point of banality. More and more people are subscribing to the Internet. The President and Vice President lead discussions on the forthcoming Information Superhighway and multinational corporations are busily jockeying for their slices of the pie.

With the change that occurs to individuals there is also a general effect on the culture of users at large and also an effect on how we shape the Internet. This mutual evolution shapes our society as well as the growth and direction that the Internet and the technology progress in. Just as having to redefine ourselves challenges us to be aware of ourselves, our self-definition also pushes the direction in which the Internet grows. Both the use that the Internet is put to and the uses that it would not be put to are shaped. It would be as difficult to perceive using the phone to listen to someone's radio as it would be for some people to understand Real Audio being used entirely to carry a radio signal to a computer speaker. We are in a market-driven and research-driven society. This makes customers and usage everything.

Some cultural anthropologists have examined the nature of "kids culture." There are researchers who have studied how children process information and respond to advertising. And there are psychologists who have conducted one-to-one sessions with sample groups of children. These experts have found that children, whose "learning skills are at their peak," can easily master the new media's learning curve, which is often daunting for adults (Gruen, 1995, p. 4). They also determined that the on-line world corresponds to the "four themes of childhood, namely Attachment/Separation, Attainment of Power, Social Interaction and Mastery/Learning" (*Interactive Marketing News*, 1995, n.p.). And they found that when children go online, they enter a "flow state," a "highly pleasurable experience of total absorption in a challenging activity" (n.p.). All of these factors make online media a perfect vehicle for advertising to children.

While children are struggling with issues of growing up—gaining independence, developing strength, getting along with others, and mastering new skills, their vulnerabilities are exposed. Once they identify how children use their online experience to meet developmental needs, the advertising industry is learning how to exploit children more effectively. The practices advertisers use to build relationships with children are calculated to make them believe that many of their needs can be met through their online experiences. Once children are totally absorbed in an online advertising environment, they are relatively defenseless and are good targets for all sorts of pitches.

One clue to the shape of the future lies in the way that people need to, fail to, and try to communicate with one another. Some people are convinced that spending hours a day in front of a screen, typing on a keyboard, in some way fulfills our need for a community of peers. Whether we have discovered something wonderful or stumbled into something insidious, or both, the fact that people want to use the Internet to meet other people and experiment with identity are valuable signposts to possible futures. Human behavior in cyberspace gives rise to important questions about the effects of communication technology on human values. What kinds of humans are we becoming in an increasingly computer-mediated world? How have our definitions of "community" and "human" been under pressure to change and fit into the specifications of a technology-guided civilization? In essence, what kind of people are we, and our friends, becoming? Is the aura of community an illusion? These questions have not been answered but are eminently worth asking. Is telecommunications culture capable of becoming something more than a pseudo-community, where people lack the genuine personal commitments to one another that form the bedrock of a genuine community? What many cybernauts are looking for and sometimes finding, is not just information, but access to ongoing relationships with a large number of other people. Individuals find friends and groups can sometimes find shared identities online. But are relationships as we know them even possible in a place where identities are fluid and elusive? The physical world, or "offline," is a place where the identity and position of the people you communicate with are known, fixed, and highly visual. In cyberspace, everybody is in the dark somewhat. We can exchange words, sounds, and pictures with each other. But there are no subtle glances, shrugs, or smiles. Even the nuances of voice and intonation are stripped away. We reduce our identities to words on a screen. The way we use these words and the stories we tell about ourselves is what determines our identities in cyberspace.

How will the continued growth of virtual communities promote alienation or facilitate community in our world? What social structures will dissolve? Which political forces will arise and which will lose power? In a sense, we are traveling blind into a technology-shaped future that might be very different from today's culture. Not knowing it, in our isolation, we are often lonely and hungry for intellectual and emotional companionship. The answers to the questions above, and the others that are being raised by a powerful and compelling new medium, are yet to be found.

When a group of people remain in communication with one another for an extended period of time, the question arises whether it is a community. The aggregation of these interactions with each other determines the nature of cyber-culture. Virtual communities might be real communities, pseudo-communities, or something entirely new in the realm of social contracts. Social norms and shared mental models have not emerged yet, so everyone's sense of what kind of place cyberspace is can vary widely. However, we are all in this together. The diversity of the cyberspace population is one of the defining characteristics of the medium, one of its main attractions, and the source of many of its most disturbing problems.

DEMOCRACY AND EQUALITY IN CYBERSPACE

We are in the formative stage of a new digital age. Providing access to the Internet for traditionally disenfranchised groups such as children and the underprivileged is an important concern in this time of transition. Government policies are being debated and enacted, marketing and programming strategies are being developed, and services designed for use on the Internet are being created. If we believe some hyperbolic visions of cyberspace, the Information Superhighway will become a great equalizing force that will bring unprecedented opportunity for all. Benefits to groups such as children and low-income families are part of this vision. Anyone without access to this communications system is likely to fall behind and be unable to compete in a highly selective job market. As access is becoming increasingly important, there are a number of groups that do not have access to the Internet.

History offers us cautionary lessons. In this century enthusiasts have hailed every new medium, from FM radio to television, cable to satellites with claims that these things would reinvigorate our culture, expand educational opportunities, and enhance the democratic process. None of these media have lived up to their claims. In each case, powerful commercial forces have used civic values to get the support for the new medium and then crush the very policies necessary to serve the public interest.

Children

The number of children who live in poverty, with little or no access to technology, is growing very quickly. Only a small percentage of families with incomes less than $20,000 have a computer as compared to nearly 60% of those families with incomes above $50,000. Even if more children can use the new media through their schools and libraries, they will still be at a disadvantage compared with children who have access at home. One or two hours of computer lab time in school are not enough to develop the technological competence that colleges and many jobs now require. Though some argue that the costs of the computer will continue to drop dramatically in the next few years and will make computers as affordable as televisions and VCRs, monthly service charges are also a barrier and communications services that are now free or inexpensive may be too expensive for families living in poverty.

Access isn't the only challenge for children. There are concerns about the quality of the new media culture. The media is two-way and dynamic. This participatory quality makes it very compelling to children. Such technological breakthroughs as real-time audio, real-time video and virtual reality modeling (which allows Websites to become three-dimensional pseudo-environments) is transforming online media. Eventually, this interactive world could supplant traditional media, such as television, as the most powerful and influential medium in a child's life.

There are a few Websites that can serve to enfranchise a child. These online services can challenge a child and expose him to places, people, and ideas that are outside his everyday experience. For example, "Plugged In," a Website created in Palo Alto, California lets many poor children explore the Internet, produce their own art, and display it to other children around the world. Another Website, "Cyber-Kids," lets children write and share their own stories in an online magazine. There are also special networks that foster online communities for children. In addition, the National Youth Center Network, with assistance from a federal grant, is attempting to address problems such as violent crime and unemployment by linking youth centers in low-income neighborhoods. However, these educational and civic services are in danger of being overshadowed by a commercial culture that has an unprecedented ability to capture a child's attention.

Low Income Families

In a study by the US Department of Commerce (National Telecommunications and Information Administration, 1995), American society is described as one in which an "individual's economic and social well-being increasingly depends on the ability to access, accumulate, and assimilate information" (n.p.). The report also says, "Although a standard phone line can be an individual's pathway to the riches of the information age, a personal computer and modem are rapidly becoming the keys to the vault" (n.p.). The National Information Infrastructure (NII) is described by the Clinton administration as "the most viable route to ending the differences between information haves and have-nots" (Piller, 1994, p. 91). According to Vice President Gore's vision of a fully wired society connectivity to the Information Superhighway will function as a dynamic force for social good, improving communication, education, medical care, and political participation. This kind of optimism about the ultimate impact of the Information Superhighway on low-income and racially or ethnically diverse communities is, at best, speculative. We know little about the use or value of such a resource to the "have-not" community, as this sector of the population is the least likely to be represented in today's online world. There is a widely recognized need for systematic research to determine whether connection to a global computer network will be beneficial to the so-called "information have-not" community. If the beneficial potential of public access is to be realized, it should be integrated into the working lives of users in those communities it is meant to serve.

Having determined that ideal Internet access can be an effective mechanism through which families from under-served communities may be empowered, it is necessary to identify technological and organizational strategies, tools, and models of access that are both effective and practical. If the underserved community is to share in the benefits of the Internet, they should be engaged in the access and exploration of the Web. Internet use must be implemented in ways appropriate to the context of individual users and user communities to facilitate specific goals they wish to achieve. If our society is to avoid segmentation into groups unable to communicate with each other, "the information haves" will be capable of accessing and using information electronically, and the "information have-nots" will suffer the consequences of computer network illiteracy.

There is strong evidence for the Internet's potential to empower and enrich the lives of those who access it. And although access to the Internet is readily available, such access is neither universal nor equitable. Access to and use of the Internet requires a substantial investment by the user. At a minimum, users need time to learn, understand, and navigate the Internet. The user also requires computers, modems, software, and telephone lines as well as the financial resources to pay for the recurring monthly charge associated with an Internet connection. For these reasons the economically disadvantaged are not well represented among current Internet users.

The Clinton administration has brought up the disparities between the information rich and information poor. In its 1993 Agenda for Action, the White House called for all schools, libraries, and hospitals to be connected to the National Information Infrastructure by the year 2000. The idea was to provide equal access at these institutions even if it couldn't be assured for all homes. However, there are presently only a handful of government programs created to encourage innovation and pilot projects and the administration has mostly relied on private, voluntary efforts to meet this goal. There are a few promising projects, such as California's NetDay, an effort begun in March 1996 that was spearheaded by Sun Microsystems where volunteers across the state strung miles of wire to connect elementary and secondary schools to the Internet. But relying heavily on such voluntary efforts has left many communities and schools unconnected. The majority of public schools, particularly those serving minority and low-income children, don't have the basic technology and training to provide students access to computer networks.

When the Telecommunications Act of 1996 was created, comprehensive policies for ensuring equitable access to the National Information Infrastructure could have been written into law. But because of a conservative political climate, unprecedented lobbying expenditures, and the pressure brought to bear by the telecommunications industries, which contributed heavily to campaigns, the legislation dealt very narrowly with this issue. This was a missed opportunity to make the Internet a truly democratizing influence.

"Democracy and Equality in Cyberspace" addressed the issues of access, universal service and empowerment on the Internet. It discussed the need to enfranchise groups like children and those in a low socio-economic group with Internet capability. For children, information concerning their needs for using the Web was placed within the context of home, school, and libraries. Individuals having a low socio-economic background face circumstances of access unique to their predicament. Their enfranchisement is discussed within the hierarchy of government policy and the Clinton administration's endorsement of a National Information Infrastructure.

THE PUBLIC INTEREST AND THE INTERNET

The Federal Communications Act of 1934, gave broadcasters "free and exclusive use of broadcast channels on condition that they serve the 'public interest, convenience, and necessity'" (Minow & LaMay, 1995, p. 4). Defining what constitutes the public interest has left Congress, the courts, and the FCC extremely frustrated over the years. Attempting to define this has produced the most concern in establishing educational programming for children. When addressed, the topic of how to regulate television, radio and the Internet usually turns into a debate over government censorship and the First Amendment.

Creating commercial imperatives for the regulation of television, radio and the Internet has long been a priority for broadcasters and advertisers. For example, when television was first becoming an established medium, broadcasters induced parents to purchase television sets, alluding to the high quality of children's programming. However, once advertisers and broadcasters had defined children as

targets of a consumer culture, the quality of children's programs dras-
tically declined. This prompted debate among regulators and critics
who articulated their concerns over the welfare of children. In 1961,
Newton Minow, former FCC chairman, called television "a vast
wasteland; a fallow field waiting to be cultivated and enriched"
(Minow & LaMay, 1995, p. 7). Thirty years later, Congress passed
"The Children's Television Act of 1990, which recognized children as
a special audience, and it required commercial broadcasters to provide
educational and informational programs for children" (p. 10).
However, the influence of advertisers who disguise their commercials
as mini-cartoons in hopes of marketing and selling their products to an
unsuspecting audience is still surrounding children's programming.
Commercial television and its impact on children serves as a harbin-
ger for creating a protocol addressing regulatory content for television, radio, and the Internet.

As the Internet continues to penetrate our lives, Congress has a second chance to define what Americans mean by the public interest.
Congress has an opportunity to impact the future of technology with
regard to children. According to Minow and LaMay,

> The choice is not between free speech and the marketplace on the one
> hand, and governmental censorship and bureaucracy on the other. The
> choice is to serve the needs of children and use the opportunities pre-
> sented by the superhighway in the digital age to enrich our lives.
> (Minow & LaMay, 1995, p. 15).

They also believe that if Congress fails to meet that choice, there
will be more sex and more violence in a larger wasteland than anyone
could imagine.

Defining the public interest was best expressed as an economic or
marketplace concern. Both Presidents Reagan and Bush attempted to
veto the Children's Television Act, stating that "it violated the First
Amendment and that the market should determine what children see on
television" (Minow & LaMay, 1995, p. 21). In an FCC hearing in 1994,
former FCC Commissioner, James Quello, objected to clarifying the
Commission's policies to educational and informational content. He
insisted that "the more specific we get in clarifying the rules, the closer
we are to violating First Amendment rights" (p. 106). "Should we
accept the idea that the First Amendment both prohibits us from pro-

tecting our children from the mass media and from nurturing them through the mass media?" (p. 107).

Minow and LaMay argue that the First Amendment forbids the government from interfering with free speech and protects the expression of ideas, but it does not make them all equal. The same argument can be applied to the Internet. Applying free speech principals and First Amendment law to technology cannot be expressed in the same format for children as adults. Unrelated to the First Amendment, both state and federal law recognize that there are " 'age-based distinctions' that regulate children's activities to include sexual activity, alcohol, tobacco, marriage, driving, to name a few" (Minow & LaMay, 1995, p. 120). The justification is to protect the interest of the minor. However, as we have seen, companies marketing on the Internet have had little or no regulation and are selling all types of products to children.

THE MAKING OF POLICY AND OVERSIGHT

Public policy-making in the United States involves somewhat arcane processes and procedures and a bewildering array of participants. It encompasses the implementation of governmental programs and the development of large-scale strategic designs. There is the President and Congress, their staff, committees, and councils. There is the federal judiciary at every level, uncountable departments, and other sub-units of the executive branch. There are thousands of politically active interest groups and lobbies, and the mass and communications media. There are state and local officials and their organizations, numerous quasigovernmental agencies, special authorities, and government contractors. There are even a few academics. All of these are players in the process of policy making.

Two branches of government, Congress and the Executive Branch are at the center of national policy and program development. The working relationship between the two is critical to the success or failure of U.S. policies and programs. Both play an important role in creating national policies. From the purchase of multibilliondollar weapons systems, to the control of the World Wide Web, Congress and the Executive Branch are engaged in a struggle for control of public policy. Although both branches will sometimes state the importance of cooperation in addressing the nation's challenges, differing orientations toward their respective constituencies, a need to protect political turf, partisan loyalties, and outside interests discourage that cooperation.

Over the past decade, resources for a new departure in public policy have mostly been unavailable. Caught between escalating entitlement programs like Social Security, pension programs, interest on the federal debt, and stagnant levels of federal revenues, increases in domestic programs have been scaled back. During the early 1980's, some domestic programs were cut and a few were ended altogether. With the end of the Cold War, defense programs also became subject to the constraining pressures of spiraling national budget deficits. By 1985, expensive, large-scale policy departures of any kind had become matters of rhetoric, not action.

Since the adoption of the Constitution, the history of policy and oversight has been marked by pendulum swings of government power, especially between the Legislative and Executive Branches. By constitutional design, legislative and executive powers were intended to be divided into broad mandates with respect to both policy making and administration. And throughout much of the nineteenth century, Congress often played a major role in the execution and development of public policy. Until the 1970's, government power was concentrated in the Executive Branch. However, after the Vietnam War and the Watergate scandal, Congress reacted to a public perception of growing presidential insensitivity, remoteness, and excessive power. To be more responsive, Congress added the Congressional Budget Office and the Office of Technology Assessment (OTA) to its support agencies, and increased the numbers of congressional staff and subcommittees.

Oversight

The role of congressional oversight is often misunderstood. Article I (sections 1 and 8) of the Constitution states that the central function of Congress is to legislate. Inherent in this power is the responsibility to exercise control over the agencies of the Executive Branch. The authority to determine the objectives of executive action also implies a responsibility to make sure that steps are taken to achieve those objectives. As a result, the role of congressional oversight has evolved to be an essential part of the separated and shared powers system. Congress is responsible for considering how policies are executed, whether they achieve the results intended, and the action that should be taken if the results are not achieved.

Observers in government lament over a legislature that places an abundance of structures on direct government operations. According to these views, multiple control systems, personnel ceilings and freezes, budget austerity, and a host of other rigid administrative requirements have robbed executive managers of the flexibility and discretion necessary for effective performance. It is argued that such constraints coupled with judicial restrictions, and requirement on executive performance has led to a managerial paralysis and the inability of government to do its work. Congress's role of lawmaking, oversight, and representation has become blurred and it is often difficult to distinguish between its role and its responsibility.

Congress has not performed a comprehensive examination of how it conducts oversight for at least a decade. Despite its mandate to "exercise continuous watchfulness of the execution of the administrative agencies" and repeated reaffirmations that "comprehensive and systematic oversight ought to be conducted," such functions have not prevailed in practice. However, with the return of divided party, control of the two branches of Congress and other forces of political, social, economic, and international change in recent years, the pendulum has swung. Congress has begun to accelerate its interest in oversight and has intervened in the details of administration.

At the present time, the FTC, which has enforcement authority over "unfair or deceptive acts or practices in or affecting commerce," is in the process of adapting and extending its regulatory reach to cover commerce conducted via email, the Web, and CD's. Email, bulletin boards, scrolling Web pages, hyperlinks, banner ads, push technology, and other features of electronic commerce have raised questions for the FTC and businesses regarding how to apply terms such as, "mail," "direct mail," and even "written." The Commission is proposing clarifications of such terms and also attempting to provide guidance regarding how disclosures should be made in electronic media advertising. Many rules recommend that material information be disclosed to consumers to prevent deception. Internet advertising contains unique features that raise new issues in making disclosures effectively. Addressing these concerns, Congress passed the 1996 Telecommunications Act establishing a broad framework for federal policy on the shape of the electronic media.

According to this Act, three goals should guide public and private policy efforts. These include:

• Insuring universal access. Every child should have access to the advanced communications technologies and services necessary for their education and full participation in society. Though access to telecommunications is not a technological quick fix for more complex social issues, the problems will only increase unless we adopt policies, and invest significant resources to ensure access for all segments of society.

• Political participation should be expanded beyond those groups that have traditionally been involved in telecommunications policy. Child advocacy, parent, health, and other constituencies need to understand what may seem to be a highly technical subject. Targeted strategic interventions at the state level could have a positive influence on local communications services. In the states, coalitions of education, consumer, and lowincome advocates can be successful in obtaining substantial resources for community computing centers, educational technology, and training.

• There should be a national movement on behalf of children's interests in the National Information Infrastructure. Public interest groups should monitor the plans of telecommunications companies to prevent "electronic redlining," or omitting lowincome neighborhoods from new initiatives. These public interest groups are defined by their agendas, which don't always agree. Some support strict censorship while others propose equality of access.

Lobbying

Lobbying organizations generally focus on building, clarifying and articulating the thoughts and feelings of various publics. They usually organize a marketing campaign to push Congress and lawmakers towards their goals or initiatives. In recent years, "cyber political strategists" have helped to develop marketing plans that bombard lawmakers with opinions and analysis of the members through e-mail. Roger Stone, the Director of The Juno Advocacy Network, a public affairs organization that targets on-line advertisements says, "Lobbyists' bread and butter comes from generating constituent mail to elected officials" (Internet Strategic Communications, 1988, n.p.). Creating an agenda for reform has become a rallying call for concerned citizens groups.

Communities across the U.S. are struggling to write Internet policies that conform to the First Amendment. Several groups and organizations, such as People for the American Way, the American Family Association, Americans for Responsible Television, and the Children's

Advertising Review Unit (CARU) are confronting free speech, censorship, and indecency issues related to children's advertising. Groups such as these are sometimes at odds. However, protecting children is generally agreed upon as the theme of their campaigns.

The emerging media environment should serve children not only as consumers, but as citizens. While a number of exciting services for children are available on the Internet, they may disappear or be overshadowed by an all-pervasive commercial culture that will capture and dominate children's attention. Since current trends suggest that the dominant method of financing the new media is likely to be advertising, we need to make sure that noncommercial educational and informational services for children are also made available. Just as we have public spaces, playgrounds, and parks in our natural environment, we should also have public spaces in the electronic environment, where children will be able to play and learn without being subject to advertising, manipulation, or other forms of exploitation.

Relying on industry self-regulation will have little impact unless there is effective government oversight and enforcement. Screening software programs, such as Net Nanny, Cyber Patrol, and SafeSurf, might allow parents to screen out certain content areas or restrict the information that children can give out, but these tools are not very efficient, or sufficient to the challenge at hand. Children are a vulnerable audience and effective legal safeguards are necessary to prevent advertisers from manipulating children and to protect them and their families from invasions of privacy. In addition, parents must become more involved, and take greater care to find out and monitor what their children are doing.

The Center for Media Education and the Consumer Federation of America have urged the FTC to develop guidelines for advertising to children in cyberspace. These rules would restrict the collection of personally identifiable information and would require the disclosure of data collection practices on all Websites directed at children. Also, the FTC should require a clear separation between content and advertising in online services targeted at children. These rules should also apply to the interactive television services under development.

The global nature of the Internet also calls for international efforts to develop standards for new media programs and services targeted at children. Since many countries already have stricter policies for protecting children than we do, international guidelines could raise the standards for children's interactive media in the United States.

CHAPTER 5

The Web: Its Future Direction and Focus

The Internet is changing the lifestyles of most Americans and is becoming an important influence in our society. Unlike print, which took hundreds of years to influence our culture, and television, which gradually affected us more and more over the course of several decades, the impact of computers and the Internet is affecting us over a much shorter period of time.

The Internet and its exploding multimedia sector, the World Wide Web, are rapidly becoming vital links to the world's commerce, communication and culture. These communications technologies are having a significant impact on the global economy, employment opportunities, education, health care and the quality of life. More than half of new jobs today already require possession of information and technological literacy. Increasingly, smaller percentages of young people entering the labor market have the skills required for most entry-level jobs. Integrating computers into the curriculum will be essential in order to equip students for the new world of work. Those without this ability are likely to fall behind and be unable to compete in a very selective job market and be at risk for poverty.

As this media assumes a greater role in our lives, there is the danger that many children and families will be cut off from it. There are many children who cannot afford even the most basic tools of modern communication. Of the growing number of poor families with young children, as many as 30% have no phone service. As more advanced forms of communication emerge, it is likely that this gap will increasingly widen between the "information rich" and the "information poor."

The unique features of the Internet and its technology make it much more powerful than television: its potential impact on a child's development is thus substantially greater. For example, some software programs use artificial intelligence to track how a child thinks and feels. These programs can monitor every computer move that a child makes and create personalized content that is specifically designed for that child.

There already exists a powerful electronic commercial culture with the ability to capture a child's attention and invade his privacy. Unlike television, the early development of which was at least partially shaped by a mandate to serve the public interest, the Internet is developing without any regulatory restraint and little public accountability. Children are a disproportionately important market for this interactive media. They are "early adopters" of high-tech products, are more comfortable than most adults with computers, and have increasing amounts of discretionary spending power.

For example, the video game market represents one of the challenges we face. Though video games have interactive properties, engaging graphics, and can be powerful educational tools, nearly half of all video games produced in the U.S. offer violent content. It seems increasingly clear that media violence is not good for children. Researchers increasingly argue this to be true based on an accumulation of scientific research indicating that media violence can be very harmful to children. (See Annotated Bibliography for sources). Since video games not only show violent acts but also engage the players in perpetrating them, their detrimental impact can be much greater, as recent studies have already documented. Despite the introduction of ratings, violent content continues to pervade the video game market and the level and intensity of the violence is increasing. There is concern that this will remain a problem as the future unfolds.

Also, it is expected that there will be an explosion of new online services for children, many using virtual reality, 3-D animation and tracking systems with the ability to develop individualized "psychological profiles." Some sites, like the one for "Jolt Cola," send children on virtual scavenger hunts across the Web, tracking the young computer user across multiple sites. "Chef Boyardee's" site invites children to become a part of its advertisements by having them rearrange storyboards for television promotions. And there is "Madeleine's Mind," a cyber serial created by Digital Planet designed to allow sponsors to place their products within the storyline. Other companies are beginning to experiment with advertising "Robots." These robots have been called Gamebots, Roverbots, Clonebots, Warbots, Spybots and even Barneybots. They can be given personalities and can even evolve and replicate themselves. Togglethis, a New York based company, has pioneered a new software called Interactive Character Technology, which creates animated characters that live on a child's PC, react to his actions and behave according to instructions received remotely. Recently, Bozlo Beaver made its dèbut and is sure to be followed by other interactive characters. These trends in the development of interactive content raise serious issues about the quality of our children's electronic future. If allowed to develop without any form of intervention, a manipulative, intrusive and even pernicious media culture could develop.

As the Internet evolution grows, it is expected that all countries around the world will increasingly get involved in it. The world community will likely form a group that will make major decisions and set Internet standards. It is also likely that the Internet will become many things—a global mall, a global research center, or a global town square. Though it is the hope that everyone on earth will use the Internet eventually, this is not necessarily what will happen. Today, as much as 25% of all the countries worldwide have high-tech technology while the rest lives in starvation. Though the Internet will be an Information Superhighway, the information it disseminates and the types of information available will not be available to everyone. There will be attempts to provide security in regards to personal information privacy. And attempts will be made to create international laws to protect everyone's private information on a worldwide scale. Nations will seek ways to cooperate in this process.

The global nature of the Internet will require international efforts to develop standards for new media programs and services targeted at children. No doubt competing interests will influence the future direction of the Internet. For example, debate over the issues of free speech, consumer privacy, and the protection of children will likely continue. And though competing interests will jockey for position, they may ultimately seek accommodation with one another.

While there has been a great deal of commotion about how the new technologies will benefit children's lives, it is still too early to determine whether that promise will be fulfilled. Although there are thousands of products and services already on the market, we are still in the very early stages of this new digital age. The contours of the new media landscape are just now becoming visible. No one yet knows what the full range of products and services for children will be, which ones will be successful, or how children will ultimately use and interact with these technologies.

There is a danger that the publishers, toy manufacturers, and new media giants who dominate the children's market will use the new technologies to simply add a veneer of interactivity or a dash of intelligence to maintain their market share. A more lifelike, talking Barbie is unlikely to be any less shallow and stereotypical than the original. There is no guarantee that the flashiest, most interactive Websites will offer anything more than a diversionary value to children.

The educational software market already shows evidence that the reality of children and computers often falls far short of the ideal. Every year, millions of dollars are spent on computer hardware and software for homes and schools. Parents rush to buy home PCs and load them with educational software, hoping that their children won't fall behind or be less prepared for school than their classmates. However, we tend to teach children how to use computers, not as a means for exploration, self-expression, and creativity, but as an end in itself. Many of the "educational" games offered are geared toward drills and memorization and lack the flexibility in design to adapt to children with different abilities and learning styles. These educational 'tools' focus on time-oriented game play where beating the clock, or conquering opponents, is the primary goal. Although some educational software companies (i.e., Edmark, MECC, and Broderbund) have pioneered a more open-ended approach to game play, the vast majority of children's titles continues to follow the same basic—and not especially creative—format.

THE ACCELERATING PACE OF LIFE IN THE FUTURE

Technology speeds up everything. If a new method of technology gets the same result with less effort, someone will introduce it. If you aren't inclined to switch over to the new technique, your competitor will, and you will have to follow suit. Otherwise, your competitor will gain an edge, producing more than you for the same investment. This competitive drive leads to a frantic chase for more efficient methods and optimization of existing systems. It pushes researchers to develop even more powerful technologies. Diminishing effort also means diminishing the time needed to get the desired result. Why spend days on a task that can be performed in hours? You can use the time gained to produce more of the same, to tackle different problems, or simply to relax. Technological innovation leads directly to speeding up of existing processes. With improved technology, houses will be built, motorcars will be assembled, food will be produced, and diseases will be cured in less time than it used to take.

This acceleration is even more striking in the distribution of information. In pre-industrial times, people communicated over long distance by letters, carried by couriers on horseback. Present-day-modems, through which computers can communicate over telephone lines, can transmit messages around the world at rates exceeding 56,000 bits per second. Powerful long-distance connections that use fiber-optic cables transmit 300 million bits per second. Over the last 200 years, the speed of information transmission has increased 10 billion times. And this is only the beginning! Experiments with even higher transmission rates are going on. The acceleration of data transmission is significant because it also boosts scientific and technological progress. The fast transmission of information is eliminating a major bottleneck of scientific innovation, since the delay between the time an idea is written down and the time it is read by another scientist is nearly nil. A researcher can make a document, including all relevant data, illustrations and references, announce its availability to hundreds or thousands of scientists and start getting their reactions within the next few hours.

Readiness is a key term associated with a child's ability to learn. In our society, parents have placed a premium on this and have hastened a child's ability to read and write. The quick pace with which we expect children to adapt and learn has a profound effect on child development. Instant gratification and rewards are influencing the way our children interact and behave. Clearly, accelerating fulfillment can have a negative impact on children. Negative characteristics associated with hedonistic need-fulfillment may include a shortened attention span, limited tolerance and patience, and reliance on less challenging problem solving skills. The accelerated pace of the Internet and its dizzying fulfillment of need can create a contradiction of sensibilities related to emotional equilibrium. Are we creating a more stressful environment for our children and a less compassionate sense of reality? Is the lack of compassion accelerating the learning curve and generating greater tension?

The Web's Role in Shaping, Manipulating and Constructing the Future

An important clue to the shape of the future might be found in the way people communicate with each other. Some people believe that spending hours a day in front of a screen fulfills our need for a community of peers. The fact that people want to use the Internet to meet others is a signpost to a possible future. Human behavior in cyberspace gives rise to important questions about the effects of communication technology on human values. What kinds of humans are we becoming in an increasingly computer-mediated world and do we have any control over that transformation? Have our definitions of "human" and "community" been under pressure to change to fit the specifications of a technology-guided civilization? Many of us are increasingly sitting in front of the computer. The question is what kind of people are we becoming? When people lack genuine personal commitments to one another, is this merely a "pseudo-community" or is the idea of "genuine" changing in an age where more of us live our lives in an increasingly artificial environment? The physical world or "off-line," is a place where the identity and position of the people we communicate with are well known, fixed, and highly visual. In cyberspace, everybody is in the dark. Usually, we only exchange words with each other. There are no glances, few nuances of voice and intonation, and there is a lack of human touch and real connection. Our identities are reduced to words on a screen. The way we use these words and what we tell about ourselves, is what determines our identities in cyberspace.

If a group of people are in communication with one another for an extended period of time, does this create a community? A virtual community can either be a real community or a pseudo-community. Whether real or pseudo, it is a desire for community in the aftermath of traditional communities and their disintegration around the world. Our sense of what kind of place cyberspace is and will be varies from one individual to the next. However, the diversity of the cyberspace population is one of the defining characteristics of the medium. It is one of the chief attractions and the source of many of its problems. In a sense, we are all in this together, yet the virtual community can both facilitate "community" and promote "alienation." Will some of our most cherished social structures dissolve? Will other new ones arise? What political forces will develop and which ones will lose their power? In a sense, we are blind travelers in a technology-shaped environment that might be very different from today's culture.

The hypothesis that humanity is evolving into a global society implies that an economic, political, cultural and technological integration is occurring among the peoples of the world. And yet there are counter-movements of nationalism, religious fundamentalism, and cultural separatism which oppose the development of a world community. Are the cities of the world falling apart, or are we witnessing a new renaissance of city life and development which is only beginning to unfold?

Given the rapid technological and social changes occurring in the world today, humanity is being moved toward significant adaptive changes. However, we are not simply passive pawns in the process of change. We are guiding the changes occurring around us and we can also guide the changes within ourselves. Some farsighted thinkers believe that the natural process of evolution can be guided and enhanced. They also believe that we are participants in the evolutionary process and we cannot completely control or predict the direction of change.

Change is, of course, a critical commodity to the growth of children. Environmental and technological variables impact upon them in numerous ways. Their lives are mediated by a host of influences that can only be measured in increments defined by cultural imperatives. The Internet and its effect as a tool for growth and maturation on children is paramount to this discussion. How it influences a child's chronological evolution and intellectual development remains an important area of study for the future.

VIRTUAL CONSTRUCTS AND THE PERCEPTION OF REALITY IN THE FUTURE

On May 7, 1987, Proctor and Gamble Corporation submitted Olestra, a new food substitute, to the FDA for approval. In the judgment of the world's media, Olestra was potentially one of the most significant nutritional breakthroughs of its time. It promised what every dieter wanted, the realization of an impossible dream: fat-free fat. Olestra is made out of sugar and fat. However, when chemically bonded in the proper way, the two form a new substance, sucrose polyester. Sucrose polyester retains the culinary and textural qualities of fat, but in a form the body is unable to digest. This results in a fat that passes straight through the body. In tests of obese subjects who ate a diet using Olestra, they lost weight. Soon after Olestra's announcement, a group called the Center for Science in the Public Interest, quoted tests that showed nearly half the rats fed on Olestra died.

What are the extent and limits of the artificial? Is there any contact with reality when it is possible to make fat that is not fat, when the fake becomes indistinguishable and even more "authentic" than the original? How do we protect ourselves from this kind of artificial reality?

Products like Olestra make it difficult to distinguish between real and unreal. Fat-free fat, alcohol-free alcoholic drinks, sugar-free sweets, and caffeine-free coffee, all suggest that you cannot have something for nothing, that everything has its price, that nothing in life is free and that there can be no gain without some pain. However, the food of which dieters dream of is fast becoming a reality. A few cancerous rats don't prove anything and there is no law of science that says fat-free fat is impossible. It is this kind of debate and a feeling of uncertainty in what we can believe that makes the idea of reality more difficult. As the unreal is continually being realized, it becomes more difficult to hold a clear view distinguishing reality and fantasy.

Throughout the industrialized era and increasingly more so today, there is no secure view of reality. Industry and the power to manufacture what had previously been taken from nature, has made the world progressively more artificial and less real and has gradually replaced the natural world with one of our own making. When the newspapers and food manufacturers tell us that dreams are fast becoming realities, does that mean that reality is becoming a dream?

At a virtual reality conference in England, during the summer of 1991, the Chairman of the Conference, Tony Feldman, observed that technology could manipulate reality to the point of being able to create it. In a sense, artificialization had become real and for this reason reality could no longer be considered secure or even assumed to be there. In the world of virtual reality, technology provides an intimate 'interface' between humans and computer imagery. It offers a simulation of the full ensemble of the senses that make up a "real" experience. The term "artificial reality" has a more technological label. Its advocates offer not only the promise of a world where you can eat fat without getting fat, but the creation of any world you could ever imagine or want. The idea of artificial reality may even reveal that much of what we take to be real is myth, just as Olestra tries to show the idea of fat as a myth. It shows that the things we assume to be independent of us are actually constructed by us. The idea of "real" has become a marketing term for business.

Today, we are in the midst of an artificial reality, one surrounded by the constructions of commerce and culture. Virtual realists think they can make something better, and that dreams can truly be turned into reality. What has happened is that we have begun to have difficulty distinguishing between simulation and imitation, artificial and virtual, unreal and real. In American culture, the essence of fantasy has been a theme associated with children and their need for nurturance. From "Grimm's Fairy Tales" to videos of "Aladdin" and theatrical portrayals of "The Lion King" and "Beauty and the Beast," our society has perpetuated a mythology of reality. Children are persuaded to conceptualize a reality that is artificially created and designed to assuage their perceived needs. The Internet has created a new "field of dreams" for children who have long faced the dilemmas raised by a world of conspicuous consumption. On the World Wide Web, children have the opportunity to fulfill their greatest desires as they place them within the context of fantasy and reality. What is real for children on the Internet is a virtual landscape punctuated by a "caravan of dreams." How will this affect the psychological makeup of our children and their future?

PREDICTING THE DIRECTION OF THE FUTURE

Given the acceleration of change, predicting the future is more difficult than ever. If we try to look ahead more than a decade or so, the crystal ball gets cloudy. Yet, people have always felt the need to know where they are going. Every culture has its own stories and myths about the future, whether it is the coming of the Messiah or the Last Judgment. In our own technological society, this role has been played out mostly in science fiction. Since Jules Verne and H.G. Wells, scientists, writers and artists have tried to imagine the world of the future. Their visions usually fall in between one of two broad streams—optimism and pessimism. The optimists believe that progress will continue to make life better. The pessimists believe that problems are intrinsic to humanity and that science can only aggravate them, unleashing dark forces that can forever escape control. An early and classic example of the latter view is Mary Shelley's novel *Frankenstein*. The scientist Frankenstein, in his investigation of life and death, creates a monster which he cannot keep under control. The monster escapes and terrorizes the community, only to return and destroy its creator.

New Age prophets have adopted ideas from various mystical traditions, including Buddhism, Yoga, and Shamanism, and from different "alternative" approaches, like parapsychology, tarot, crystal healing and homeopathy. This is a worldview combining science and mysticism. In this view humanity is quickly moving towards a higher level of consciousness that will transcend individual awareness and selfish concerns and be replaced by a transpersonal experience of belonging to a larger whole. Then there is the theme of a technologically controlled, bureaucratic society, where there is no room for freedom or individual expression. This theme returns in novels and movies, such as George Orwell's *1984* or Terry Gilliam's satire, *Brasil*.

A recent pessimistic vision of the future combines a focus on sophisticated cybernetic technology in a society that describes unbridled capitalism. Here everybody competes with everybody, and the gap between the "haves" and "have-nots" has become much wider. The unimaginable wealth of top business executives contrasts with the poverty of most of humanity. Technology is omnipresent as a means of control by multinational corporations. Direct brain-to-computer interfaces, global networks and mind-altering drugs are commonplace. Everybody is either vying for control, or trying to escape the harsh reality in computer-generated fantasy worlds. But no one is really in control. The technology-driven society is simply too complex for anybody to grasp. The continuing uncertainty and fight for survival has eroded any sense of justice, values, or ethics, replacing them by a high-tech variant of the law of the jungle. In this scenario, I cannot help but be reminded by the concentration camps of Auschwitz, Dachau, Birkenau, and the others, where technology was used to nearly obliterate a people, and in a sense, our own humanity.

Predicting the future reveals the fallibility of prediction as well as a history of human hopes and fears. Even the most flawed or utopian dream offers insights into how people thought about their world, about social change, about themselves, and about their technology. Predicting the future always reflects the experience of the moment as well as memories of the past. They are imaginary constructs that have more to say about the times in which they were made than about the real future, which is, ultimately, unknowable. Many predictions have been exaggerated, wrong or utopian. And many predictions are related to the popularity of a particular belief as well as their consequences. In the 1950's, there were some thinkers who believed that nuclear energy would supplant other sources of power. They prophesized atomic-powered automobiles and washing machines. These enthusiasts failed to foresee the problems of developing nuclear energy. Safety hazards were underrated and the ability to which reactors might be made smaller and lighter was overrated. It was also not understood that new innovations seldom become universal overnight.

The history of science and technology shows us that only over time and through prolonged use are complex devices sufficiently improved to find widespread application. And through such use, problems not initially envisioned often emerge to slow the acceptance of the technology, such as what to do with all the atomic waste generated by nuclear technology. The builders of the first digital computers predicted that the machine would be a "super-calculator" that would solve complex scientific equations. They did not imagine computers being used in wholly different social contexts and functions, such as business use, word processing, or graphics design. Electric light aroused similar utopian expectations. For thousands of years, it was thought that only G-d could have invented light and would rescue humanity from darkness. It is not surprising that this technology had a messianic promise and was greeted as a force for universal betterment. The same is true today. Some of us believe that the best indicator of future behavior is past behavior. In that vein, a media that entertains does not necessarily teach and advertisements do not necessarily sway the consumer. Though advertisers are interested in selling a product, children may be more interested in the problem-solving process rather than the product itself.

Perhaps we can view the computer and the Internet as a reconstitution of the Rosetta Stone. It just could be the key for children to move onto a higher dimension of thought and perception. Children and their ability to learn have been completely changed by computers. We have entered a new construct in the educational process that has moved learning from a passive to an active state. Are we to relinquish control of our children's development and hand it over to the mediated culture of advertising? Or is control only an artificial construct reverting back to a culture immersed in a philosophy that is out of date? Is morality lost to technology and will our children lose a sense of justice and ethics? In the final analysis, we do not know what the future will bring. All we can really do here is speculate.

CHAPTER 6

The Web: Tool or Trap?

There is a Hindu proverb that states, "You never bathe in the same river twice." The meaning of it is that things move and change is inevitable. And whenever something new is discovered, or invented, or marketed, at that very second everything else becomes outdated.

There is no doubt that we cannot turn back: the genie is out of the bottle, and the Internet is here to stay. What we choose to do about that irrefutable fact, and how we address the complex issues it is raising, particularly in regards to children, will have a great deal of impact on whether or not this new medium is a blessing or a bane. We know from past experience that mass media is powerful, and that its power can be directed in ways that are either positive or negative. As we grapple with the issues of yet another new medium, the lessons of the past can guide us into our future.

• The Internet can become another wasteland much like television has become.
• Children's behavioral development can be adversely affected by this medium.
• Perceptions of self and reality may negatively affect children's values and ethics.

Examining the Internet as a social and political force in American society yields a number of challenges. As a relatively new area of research, the methodology for identifying trends and issues is without established guidelines. Though attempts have been made to compare the Internet with other media such as television and radio or the computer in general, such comparisons may not be accurate or adequate. Therefore, as a relatively new discipline of study, the Internet and its impact on children and society offers a unique opportunity for scholarly pursuit. In any case, there is an urgent need to conduct further research in the following areas:

• How children react to virtual worlds.
• How learning is assimilated from the Web by children.
• How advertisers use Websites to attract children.
• How the written word and narrative structure are being redefined and affected by this new medium.
• What physical anomalies and injuries Internet use is having on children over time.
• Whether children are being more or less "interconnected" as a result of Internet use.

Today's children face a bewildering proliferation of technologies in a new media environment. The World Wide Web holds great promise for improving their lives. There are online and interactive services which could spawn a bright new array of offerings. Ready to Learn Web Channels, and health networks could build on the best traditions in educational programming. Telecommunications links could also enhance classroom learning, and connect children to vast educational resources around the world.

But there is a great risk that the promise will not be met for all children and many of them will not be able to participate fully in this Digital Age. If current trends continue, the gap between the "information rich" and "information poor" could widen dramatically. This, of course, is an issue closely associated with the Internet as a tool for enfranchisement. Without meaningful access to the new communications system, many children could find themselves cut off from society, missing out on educational opportunities, and unprepared for the job market in the 21st century. There is also a danger that educational and civic media could be overshadowed by a darker electronic world of exploitation and over-commercialization. Video games could pipe a stream of violent images into our homes. New forms of interactive advertising, disguised as information or entertainment, could manipulate children and invade their privacy in addition to collecting vast amounts of personal information.

Unlike any other type of communication medium, children find the interactive nature of online services extremely compelling. No other medium lets you exchange e-mail communications instantaneously, make new friends anywhere in the world, or participate in chat rooms about the very subjects that interest you more than anything else. The culture that once depended on society to write letters, talk on the telephone, and watch television has been transformed to e-mail addicts. According to Wendy Lesser, author of *The Conversion*, "Your e-mail address becomes a part of your permanent identity in a way that no mere phone number can" (Birkets, 1996, p. 125). This, of course, has implications for the future of free speech, privacy, and self-determination.

It is still not certain whether the same oversight that prevails with content regulation and other media also applies to the Internet. The Internet is used to promote other forms of communication— to broadcast radio, movies, and to make international phone calls. As the FTC outlines its guidelines for children's advertising and content, it has become a difficult task to try and restrict certain advertisements for children. The technical improvements that have been suggested seem to involve complicated software that will enable parents to only partially block out sites. And before we can establish legal parameters for regulating children's content and advertising, Congress must decide how to define the Internet as a global form of communication. Issues concerning unfair advertising content toward children have been addressed by the FTC and are an important factor in developing public policy.

Television helped transform the American political and cultural landscape. Today, parents, educators, cultural critics and lawmakers are grappling with the force and influence of the Internet. As might be expected, we look for lessons or parallels with television as an example of having a similar effect. Television has had a mixed record. On the one hand, it has been a powerful tool for educating and informing vast numbers of the American public, drawing together disparate groups into a common collective experience. On the other hand, it also has been accused of pandering to the lowest of human urges, cheapening and coarsening our cultural fabric. Despite decades of scientific research on its effects and vigorous public debate, violent images continue to intrude into our daily lives. Children's programs have become little more than 30-minute commercials for toys and other "licensed" products. Might the Internet be no different?

The explosion of communications technologies will shape children growing up today. Certainly, Piaget's theories about child development and how children respond to advertising are germane to the affect of communications technologies on child behavior. His delineation of the stages of development and the formation of cognitive growth are critical to understanding how technology molds children.

The growth of the World Wide Web, the proliferation of cable and satellite channels, and the innovation in virtual reality and 3-D modeling software, are all combining to create a compelling and pervasive interactive media environment. As the 21st century unfolds, we can only glimpse at the electronic future for our children and their generation. Every part of their daily lives will be connected to a vast digital universe that will transcend the home, the community and even the nation. The television, the computer and the telephone will continue to merge. And new personal and portable technologies will make it possible for children to inhabit their own separate electronic worlds. This stage of media convergence is especially pertinent to children and their interactive and adaptive behavior. It provides a rationale for the ways in which children use the Internet as a tool of inquiry.

The inherent properties of these multimedia technologies, their dazzling graphics and engaging interactivity, will make them potent forces in our children's future. If harnessed properly, they could benefit children in fundamental ways like enhancing their natural drive to learn, providing them with access to a rich diversity of information and ideas, and enabling them to forge links across community and national borders. But this new electronic world may hold peril as well as promise. This is exemplified by parameters that historically have sensitive cultural imperatives. Internet subscribers have not forsaken attitudes related toward race, sexuality and gender, and low socio-economic groups. For example, technological anonymity has allowed for the harassment of women and the newly promulgated advertising of hate on the Web. As global community evolves, McLuhan (1989) stated that human culture will be transformed into an electronic global environment dominated by multimedia. The effect of the Internet on our culture will permeate every aspect of community, including language and identity.

The media of the 21st century is still in its formative stages. Marketing and programming strategies are still being developed and refined, services targeted at children are now being designed and put into place, and government policies are now debated and enacted at both the state and federal levels. The electronic future poses complex questions of equity, content, and quality that our society has never faced before. These issues are implicitly associated with children's advertising and its place in a child's electronic toy chest. Advertisers have traditionally exploited children disguising their merchandising as entertainment or educational. The Internet is also a purveyor of disguised marketing utilizing Web media. How these issues are addressed will affect children for generations to come.

There are cultural and psychological consequences of this medium that have yet to be researched and discussed. The use of advertising may be a window as to how this process is unfolding. The Internet may become ubiquitous and play a powerful role in children's lives. But children won't necessarily become smarter or more creative. Sitting in front of a computer monitor will not necessarily help them to become critical thinkers or cooperative learners. However, if used wisely and creatively, computers and related technology have the power to open up new worlds of exploration, unleashing talents that many children otherwise might never have pursued. The interactive nature of the Web creates an unusually compelling environment for learning. Whether this learning is positive or negative has yet to be determined.

High-tech toys, for all of their novelty and flash, add little of value and substance to children's lives. The tools children have access to must allow them to express themselves creatively, and give them the opportunities to explore the world around. The technology we are developing must encourage children to see themselves not as isolated individuals working at separate machines, but as part of a larger community, using high-tech tools for communication and cooperation.

We are in the midst of a fundamental transformation from an industrial society to an information society. Our economy, our professional occupations, and our technologies are increasingly emphasizing the creation, manipulation, transmission, and selling of information. This is the era of what management guru Peter Drucker (1975) calls, the "knowledge worker." Information technology and its impact on human society, human life, and the human mind, general social changes occurring within an Information Age world, and the Communication Revolution, are all issues to consider. Also important within this area of thinking is the interaction between technology and humanity. How are information and communication machines and networks altering the human mind and human society? And how are changes in human professions, life styles, and philosophies guiding the evolution of our machines? Technology accelerates the pace of everyday life. Buckminster Fuller (1967) coined the word "ephemeralization" to describe the progressive speed at which our culture could do more with less. A task normally taking days to perform now can be completed in hours. Modems, ISDN, satellite technology, and fiber optic cable all conspire to accelerate the transmission of data. Information Age thinking and potential advances in information technology take us into a variety of philosophical and scientific issues regarding the future. Will people generate the ability of computers to think? What does it mean or prove if computers do appear to think? Will a global brain and mind emerge across the world as the Internet acquires a sufficient level of complexity and organization? Will our environment become intelligent, creative, and personalized? Is cyberspace a new level of reality? Science and technology have offered a double-edged sword of dazzling promises and terrifying possibilities. Does science and technology even provide us with an adequate framework for understanding the future? Will advancing technology rob us of our humanity? Accelerating the expectation of fulfillment may impact negatively on a child's development. Will this media have a detrimental effect on children, creating a hedonistic need fulfillment, shortened attention span, limited tolerance and patience, and less challenging problem solving skills?

Psychological and technological constructs are implicit in determining the distinctions and similarities between television and the Internet for children. Traditionally, television has been a passive medium defined by an environmental presence. Interruptions and distractions are inherently part of the viewing experience. Computer mediated viewing on the World Wide Web is an interactive experience with a clear design toward involvement. While issues of convergence between technologies is a focal point for adaptive behavior, there are essential distinctions between television viewing and interaction with the World Wide Web. The computer screen is a means for an all-consuming televisual experience transporting the viewer into a virtual landscape of experiential design. In this respect it is vastly different from television because it is more than a medium of entertainment and information; it is a technology of consumption mediated by the active presence of the viewer. If there is anything we can learn or discover, it is that the myriad variables involved in the interface between children and the Web is a complex paradigm that involves thinking in new and creative ways.

The future portends a multitude of unknowns. As it unfolds, it creates challenging dilemmas and uncharted fields of knowledge. A landscape of design has yet to be created. No one can really say what cyberspace will look like in the next 50 years. And that is because it is like a new land that has only begun to be settled, or rather created. For cyberspace is defined and delineated first and foremost by its content. And its future depends, not on our ability to police it, but on what we collectively build there that is of real value to the public and that has social benefits.

APPENDIX 1

The Legion of Decency

C urrently, the Legion of Decency is replaced by the Catholic Church's Office for Film and Broadcasting. This group remains active and continues to promote their own rating system. The ratings and their assessments are as follows:

- A-1: Morally unobjectionable or general patronage
- A-2: Morally unobjectionable for adults and adolescents
- A-3: Morally unobjectionable for adults
- A-4: For adults with reservations
- A-5: Morally objectionable in part for all
- C: Condemned

The Motion Picture Association of America has approved a current system of self-regulation by warning the public of content expected in a film. The current classification of films include the following:

- G: All ages admitted, general audiences
- PG: Parental guidance suggested, for mature audiences
- PG-13: Parents are strongly cautioned to give special guidance to children under thirteen
- R: Restricted, children under seventeen must be accompanied by a parent or other adult
- NC-17: No one under seventeen admitted

APPENDIX 2 _____

Annotated Bibliography

HISTORY OF MEDIA

There are several areas that are important to understand the theme of this text. For example, several writers discuss the history of media and advertising. In a discussion of the development of information technologies, Paul Levinson (1997), in *The Soft Edge,* traces the development of information technologies from the earliest cave drawings to computers while noting each scheme's impact on society. He also analyzes the impact of inventions like the printing press, the electric light bulb, telegraph, telephone, radio, television and computers. In addition, Nicholas Negroponte (1996), in *Being Digital,* provides an informative history of the rise of technology and a visionary insight on what "being digital" means for the future. He also describes the evolution of CD-ROMs, multimedia, hypermedia, and HDTV. In addition, Negroponte recognizes certain dangers of technological advances, such as increased software and data piracy and huge shifts in the job market that require workers to transfer their skills to the digital medium. Tim Jackson (1997), in *Inside Intel: Andy Grove and the Rise of the World's Most Powerful Chip Company,* investigates the history of the processor business as well as the secrets of Intel's success. He portrays the story of technical coups tempered by serious blunders and savage competition. The author also shows how Intel was close to ruin but was successful because it could fight back savagely and not always pleasantly. The book discusses not only Intel's technology, but also that of rivals like Motorola, Cyrex, AMD, and the PC Consortium. And finally, Richard Campbell (1998), in *Media and Culture,* provides an introduction to mass communication and mass media. He presents a cultural perspective and framework in which all media develops in order to understand the conditions of mass media and its role in our lives.

FIRST AMENDMENT AND LEGAL ISSUES

A second area researched in this text addresses First Amendment and current Legal issues. For example, in a discussion of the media and First Amendment, Patrick Garry (1996), in *Scrambling for Protection: The New Media and the First Amendment,* explains why the First Amendment should protect the electronic and print media equally. He also argues that technology and democracy can go hand-in-hand. In addition, Gary explores how new telecommunications technology is allowing more people a voice in the process of social dialogue through computer networks and bulletin boards. He also discusses how the technology impacts on the aspirations of broadcast journalists and how it should and should not be regulated in terms of the constitutional protection of free speech. Newton Minow and Craig LaMay (1995), in *Abandoned in the Wasteland: Children, Television, and the First Amendment,* argue that the First Amendment can be used on behalf of children to make sure that television nurtures rather than harms them. The book offers workable ideas for an effective policy for children to limit commercial interests that dominate programming today.

Wallace and Mangan (1996), in *Sex, Laws & Cyberspace,* address the legal issues and ethical debates around the growth of the Internet and commercial online services. The very qualities that make the Internet invaluable, such as a low-cost world-wide reach, the lack of censorship, interactivity, anonymity, and the ability to carry huge amounts of data, text, images and sounds, also make them potentially dangerous. They conclude that in order to decide how to regulate the Internet, it must also be defined. Should society and the law treat it as a broadcast medium (like TV), a communication common carrier (like the phone company) or as a print medium (like a newspaper or magazine)? The authors examine these issues and discuss the tremendous pressure on the government to regulate the industry and the far-reaching implications of judicial decisions. In *Netlaw: Your Rights in the Online World*, Lance Ross (1995) discusses some of the legal issues for users of online services, and offers reasonable assessments of copyright, precedents, laws, individual rights, and the risks of many online activities. The book discusses individual rights, issues of privacy, freedom of speech, property rights and security in the online world. In *Law of the Internet*, F. Lawrence Street (1997) has written a well-organized book about the legal aspects of the Internet. The author first defines the Internet in legal terms, describes how it is different from other media and then begins a discussion on the various legal issues involved. He discusses electronic contracts, privacy, copyright issues, defamation, crime, censorship and taxation in a clear and easy to read format. And finally, Don Pember (1993), in *Mass Media Law*, discusses the American legal system, freedom of the press, the regulation of advertising, broadcast regulation and the media. Each chapter offers historical dimensions and explanations that led up to current media regulations.

THE LEGION OF DECENCY AND THE MOTION PICTURE INDUSTRY

An additional trend in this text discusses the Legion of Decency and the Motion Picture industry. Frank Walsh (1996), in *Sin and Censorship: The Catholic Church and the Motion Picture Industry*, takes us back to the early years of the century when there was a widespread conviction that the movie theater was becoming "a primary school for criminals." Inevitably, large diocese such as Boston, Chicago, and Detroit reacted to this threat with independent censorship boards. Movie producers, in turn, adopted an industry code called the "Thirteen Points" in an effort to convince the public that the industry could censor itself. Walsh discusses the emergence of the Legion of Decency, the involvement of Vatican II and more current attempts at censorship and attempts to eliminate violence and pornography from television, radio and the Internet. He also discusses the Communications Decency Act, First Amendment issues and the V-chip, a more contemporary attempt at censorship.

Charles Lyons (1998), in *The New Censors: Movies and the Culture Wars*, provides a study of the complex ways that movies have been shaped in the years since the demise of the Hays Production Code. The text covers a wide range of movies, protests, and government actions. The author links a study of public outrage against movies to the broader culture wars over "family values," pornography, and various lifestyle issues. The book also provides a contemporary history of controversial movies and a timely discussion of how cultural politics continues to affect the movie industry.

THE FCC, FTC AND THE FDA

In order to understand the continued development of regulatory practices, additional areas examined are the FCC, the FTC, and the FDA. The FCC provides extensive documentation of its policies and rules on its Internet site (http://www.fcc.gov). The material presented at this site include information on its policy structure, the history of government efforts to promote children's educational television and FCC proceedings implementing the Children's Television Act of 1966. In addition, the FCC (1996), in *Policies and Rules Concerning Children's Television,* conducted a study of 1400 Websites and found that 85 percent of them collect personal information but only 14 percent give any notification of what they do with the data. In summary, the FCC concluded that there is a need for increased efforts to build privacy protections into Internet Commerce.

Policy issues of the FDA are discussed by William Patrick (1988), in *The FDA.* Patrick provides a discussion of the FDA and the implication of its policies to business as well as to the consumer. The FDA also maintains a Website (http://www.FDA.gov) which provides information regarding all of their policies and regulations. In addition, The FTC's (1978) *FTC Staff Report on Television Advertising to Children* addresses the large volume of advertising directed to children and then begins to identify and discuss a broad range of remedies to undo the harms that come out of television advertising. The report also discusses a series of recommendations that might be considered in dealing with the problem.

CHILDREN'S CONTENT

An additional area of research addresses Children's Content. Kunkel, D. & Gantz, W. (1992), in *Children's Television Advertising in the Multicultural Environment,* examined the nature and number of commercials during children's programs on three different types of channels: broadcast networks, independent stations and cable networks. Clear patterns of differences were found across the various channel types. The broadcast networks provided the greatest amount of advertising; cable presented significantly less. Cable presented the widest range of products advertised. The study also examined the themes employed in the commercials, disclosures/disclaimers used, and other content attributes of advertising. A prominent area in children's advertising with respect to media issues and the Internet is the relationship of gender and role models. Lois Smith (1994), in *A Content Analysis of Gender Differences in Children's Advertising,* found that children's advertisements featuring characters of only one sex portrayed traditional stereotypes for male/female roles. Most traditional male/female role expectations emerged in the way advertisements were positioned. Girls stayed at home, boys roamed the world. Children see a tremendous number of advertisements each year. This, along with the propensity that children show to imitate same-sex models, indicates that advertisers have a tremendous impact on the shaping of children's behavior. According to Smith, the presence of advertising is not the problem. Advertising brings a wealth of information to children and is part of our culture. Smith concludes that the problem is in the absence of competing messages and values concerning sex roles. Ads do not portray boys as nurturing or sharing. What of the boy who could play a different role? Commercial messages often show them to be aggressive, physically active and needing to win. Just as girls should not be limited to their homes, boys should be allowed to be kind and sharing.

An area of particular concern that also has important implications is violence on television and the movie industry. Madeline Levine (1996), in *Viewing Violence: How Media Violence Affects Your Child's Development,* looks at television and movie violence in the United States. She analyzes the results of over four decades of research on the effects of media violence. Levine first points out that children at different stages understand and experience the world in very different ways.

She shows that a movie that might be instructive for an eleven-year-old could be traumatic and overwhelming for a seven-year-old. Levine concludes that media violence is not a trivial issue. Though parents are often surprised at what children might find upsetting, our society is increasingly at risk for higher levels of violence as well as for a greater tolerance and acceptance of this violence.

EFFECTS OF ADVERTISING ON CHILDREN

The effects of advertising on children is an additional area researched in this text. In *Life on the Screen,* Sherry Turkle (1995), a Harvard Psychologist, examines how human-computer interaction, especially as related to the Internet, has shaped our perception of self. The author discusses how one's view of a computer has changed from being "linear" and a tool for mathematical computations to being "non-linear" and a tool for simulation and surface exploration. She then shows that computers seem "alive" to its users and that children are today used to dealing with computers that react "intelligently." After discussing how users interact and sometimes become emotionally involved with their computers, she then discusses what she refers to as "Artificial life" or the nature of an artificial personality independent of its residence in a human being. Finally, she examines how computer–based environments influence our sense of self and our ability to reveal aspects of our personalities on a computer that would otherwise not come to the surface. Gene Del Vecchio (1997), in *Creating Ever-Cool: A Marketers Guide to a Kid's Heart,* discusses the timeless truths of children, their emotional needs, and about advertising brands that have attempted to satisfy them year after year. This book also provides a "glimpse on the inside" for the general reader, while providing vital tools for the marketer. In their quest for kids' dollars, companies market their products as not only necessary, but popular—or cool—to varying degrees of success. Some achieve tremendous success. The author offers a formula for achieving Ever-Cool success to marketers everywhere.

Clara Ferguson (1975), in *Preadolescent Children's' Attitudes Toward Television Commercials,* using a questionnaire given to 266 fourth- and sixth- grade students from schools in Salt Lake City, Utah, found that negative attitudes to television commercials increase with age. She concluded that attitudes to commercials tend to be negative at higher stages of cognitive development and tend to be positive at lower stages of cognitive development. In addition, significant proportions of pre-adolescent children doubt the validity and truthfulness of commercials. Ferguson concluded that commercial advertisers and networks need to take into account the attitudes of pre-adolescent children to commercials if television were to remain an effective advertising medium. And Brian Young (1990), in *Television Advertising and Children,* examines children's understanding of advertising, the effects of advertising on children, and the skills necessary to become "literate" in advertising. He argues that the predominant view of the "advertiser-as-seducer," and the "child-as-innocent," is a limited view. He proposes a model of advertising from current linguistic theory. Further, he concludes that research in advertisement should include psychological theories from development psychology. He also suggests intervention strategies that are helpful to children in enhancing their ability to understand advertising rather than imposing stringent regulations on advertisers.

Marketing

An additional area researched addresses marketing issues and their implications. Stephen Kline (1993), in *Out of the Garden: Toys, TV and Children's Culture in the Age of Marketing,* details a history of marketing to children and how the design of toys has had a powerful impact on the way children play. He also shows how the opportunity to reach large audiences of children through television was a pivotal point in developing new approaches to advertising. Kline also discusses how the deregulation of advertising in the U.S. in the 1980's has led to the development of new marketing strategies which have saturated the market with promotional "character toys." Finally, Kline asks whether we should allow our children's play culture to be primarily defined and created by marketing strategies and where images of real children have all but been eliminated from narratives about the young. Ellen Seiter (1993), in *Sold Separately: Children and Parents in Consumer Culture,* discusses marketing issues with reference to middle class values to children's TV and mass-market toys and then makes the association that this represents "uncontrollable consumerism" and hence a moral failure. She also states that sexist and racist views are more dangerous in the world that children's TV presents than is marketing to insatiable consumers.

Privacy and Data Collection

In the area of privacy and data collection, David Brin (1998), discusses the nature of privacy and accountability in an era of widespread surveillance technologies in his book, *The Transparent Society.* Brin speculates in considerable detail about a possible technological future. He predicts, for example, that surveillance technologies will become all-pervasive and undetectable with platforms ranging from cameras in public places to bee-like drones with inflatable lenses.

Cognitive Development

As part of his research, Jean Piaget discusses cognitive development. In *The Psychology of the Child,* Piaget (1972) synthesizes his theories of developmental psychology. In addition, he discusses the stages of a child's cognitive development from infancy to adolescence and its impact on a child. In *The Child's Conception of the World,* Piaget (1965) examines the child's view of reality and causality. He investigates the conception of the world that the child forms at different stages of his development. Also, in his 1987 work, *The Construction of the Child's Reality,* six of Piaget's central works are conceptually critiqued including the child's conception of the world, the development of morality and the origins of intelligence in infancy.

FUTURE TRENDS

The final area researched in this text looks at the future direction of advertising on the Internet. In *Web Without a Weaver: How the Internet is Shaping Our Future,* Victor Grey (1997) presents a picture of the global future being shaped by the Internet. He states that the Internet is changing our lives whether or not we ever turn on a computer and helps us understand how this is being done. In conclusion, he proposes that the Internet serves a role in the evolution of human consciousness in the way we think about ourselves and how we organize our affairs as a society. Janet Butler (1997), in *Information Technology: Converging Strategies and Trends for the 21st Century,* addresses the forces and technologies that shape the information technology industry as it moves into the 21st century. She discusses management issues, trends, products and markets concerning the computer industry. In addition, in *The Future Does Not Compute; Transcending the Machines in Our Midst,* Stephen Talbott (1995) raises questions about our machine dominated society. He states that the computer has subtle influences on us and we need to examine its implications about who we are and about our future. He further states that we must take a look at our own humanity as we embrace computer technology because the problem may be in the way we think about technology. The Renaissance National Research Council (1994), in *Realizing the Information Future: The Internet and Beyond,* uses the Internet as a springboard for a vision of the network of the future. The book discusses several components such as the National Information Infrastructure, information networks, databases, consumer electronics, and the architecture required to construct the network of the future. Finally, Douglas Robertson (1998), in *The New Renaissance: Computers and the Next Level of Civilization,* tries to convey the scope of changes that are coming while recognizing that accurate predictions are like tossing a dice. The author begins by looking at how previous, pivotal communications advancements have remade society, such as writing and printing. He then demonstrates the increasing rate of transformation brought on by computers and the dramatic change that the computer revolution is bringing. Robertson then looks at some of the potential problems that tomorrow's civilization might have to solve and how computers are capable of revolutionizing civilization. In conclusion, he presents the triumph of the human spirit as it will face the opportunities and challenges of a world transformed by computers. In his vision of the future, he also suggests that humans will be able to explore the marvels of the universe. In *Future Net,* Martin Greenberg (1996), explores some of the possibilities, perils, and challenges that the Internet may have to offer. The book provides science fiction stories about the perils and promises of the Internet. And finally, Gregory Paul (1996), in *Beyond Humanity: Cyberevolution and Future Minds,* tries to take a look at what may happen to us in the 21st century. The author begins with a discussion of Darwin and his realization that evolutionary change is the driving force in our universe. He then weaves a discussion that technological evolution will change our very minds and that we are beginning to replace ourselves with "mind" computers, or computers that think. In essence, Paul examines the possible consequences that cyber-life has for the human species.

Bibliography

Aday, S. (1996). *Newspaper coverage of children's television.* (Annenberg Public Policy Center Report No. 7). Philadelphia: University of Pennsylvania.

Alderman, E. & Kennedy, C. (1995). *The right to privacy.* New York: Knopf.

Atkin, C., & Gibson, W. (1978), Children's responses to cereal commercials (Report to Public Advocates, Inc).

Aufderheide, P. & Montgomery, K. (1994). *The impact of the Children's Television Act on the broadcast market.* Washington, DC: Center for Media Education.

Barcus, E. F. (1977). *Children's television: An analysis of programming and advertising.* New York: Praeger.

Barcus, E. F. (1983). *Images of life on children's television: Sex roles, minorities, and families.* New York: Praeger.

Barnouw, E. (1982). *Tube of plenty: The evolution of American television.* New York: Oxford University Press.

Barthel, D. (1988). *Putting on appearances: Gender and advertising.* Philadelphia: Temple University Press.

Berry, G. & Asamen, J. (1993). *Children and television: Images in a changing sociocultural world.* Newbury Park, CA: Sage Publications.

Birkets, S. (1996). *Tolstoy's Dictaphone, technology and the muse.* Minneapolis, MN: Graywolf Press.

Blank, M. (1975, March). "Eliciting verbalizations from young children in experimental tasks: A methodological note." *Child Development,* 46.

Blatt, J., Spencer, L., & Ward, S. (1971). A cognitive developmental study of children's reactions to television advertising. In E. A. Rubinstein, G. A. Comstock, & J. P. Murray (Eds.), *Television and social behavior: Vol. 4. Television in day-to-day life: Patterns of use.* Washington, DC: U.S. Department of Health, Education, and Welfare.

Brennan, M. (1997). Threat & promise, Intel Chairman Grove says Internet will alter every company career [On-line] Available: http://www.freep.com/browsing/tech/qintel//.html

Brin, D. (1998). *The transparent society: Will technology force us to choose between privacy and freedom?* Reading, Mass.: Addison-Wesley.

Britt, M., (1995, October 25). Defining the Digital Consumer IV agenda: Digital Kids pre-conference seminar. New York.

Broadhurst, J. (1993, September). "On-line gold mines: Why don't women tap into the latest business data, news and gossip?" *Working Woman,* pp. 80–81.

Brumbaugh, F. N. (1954). What effect does advertising have on children? In C. Carr (Ed.), *Children and TV.* Washington, DC: Association for Childhood Education International.

Butler, J. (1997). *Information technology: Converging strategies and trends for the 21st century.* Charleston, SC: Computer Technology Research Corporation.

Campbell, R. (1998). *Media and culture: An introduction to mass communication.* New York: St. Martin's Press.

Carter, B. T. , Dee, J. L., Gaynes, M. J., & Zuckman, H., (1994) *Mass communication law.* St. Paul, MN: West Publishing Co.

Center for Media Education. (1997). "Alcohol and tobacco on the Web: New threats to youth" [On-line].Available: http://www.tap.epn.org/cme/execsum.html

Center for Media Education. (1997). "And now a Web from our sponsor: How online advertisers are cashing in on children." *InfoActive,* 2(2), 1–10. Available: http://www.epn.org/cme/infoactive/22/22nweb.html

Center for Media Education. (1997). "CME's campaign to protect children from harmful cyber-advertising." *InfoActive,* 2(2), 1–7. Available: http://www.epn.org/cme/infoactive/22/22nweb.html

Center for Media Education. (1997). "Web of deception: Threats to children from online Marketing." *InfoActive,* Available: http://www.epn.org/cme/cmwdecov.html

Chestnut, R. W. (1979). "Television advertising and young children." *Advertising.* (July).

Civille, R. (1995). "The Internet and the poor." In B. Kahin & J. Keller (Eds.), *Public access to the Internet.* Cambridge, MA: MIT Press.

Coates, J. F. (1996). *2025: Scenarios of US and global society reshaped by science and technology.* New York: Oakhill Press.

Defleur, M. L. (1996). *Understanding mass communication.* Boston: Houghton-Mifflin.

Del Vecchio, G. (1997). *Creating ever-cool: A marketer's guide to a kid's heart.* Gretna, La: Pelican.

Donnerstein, E., Slaby, R. & Eron, L. (1994). "The mass media and youth violence." In J. Murray, E. Rubinstein, & G. Comstock (Eds.), *Violence and youth: Psychology's response.* Washington, DC: American Psychological Association.

Dorr, A. (1986). *Television and children: A special medium for a special audience.* Beverly Hills, CA. Sage Publications.

Drummond, B. (1996, July 16). "FTC outlines privacy rules for children's sites." Bloomberg News. [On-line]. Available: http://nyt.syn.com/live/News3/

Ewing, J. K. (1996). "Basing teaching on piaget's constructivism." *Childhood Education,* 72 (5).

FCC (1996). *Policies and rules concerning children's television programming: Revision of programming policies for television broadcast stations* (MM Docket No. 93–48). Washington, DC: U.S. Government Printing Office.

FTC (1978). *FTC staff report on television advertising to children.* Washington, DC: U.S. Government Printing Office.

Ferguson, C. (1975) *Preadolescent children's attitudes toward television commercials.* (Studies in Marketing No. 21). Austin: Board of Regents, University of Texas at Austin.

Flavel, J. H. (1977). *Cognitive development.* Englewood Cliffs, NJ: Prentice-Hall.

Garry, P. M. (1996). *Scrambling for protection: The new media and the first Amendment.* Pittsburgh: University of Pittsburgh Press.

Gates, B. (1995). *The road ahead.* New York: Penguin.

Gelman, R. (1978). "Cognitive development." *Annual Review of Psychology,* 29.

Goffman, E. (1979). *Gender advertisements.* New York: Harper & Row.

Goldman, R. (1992). *Reading ads socially.* New York: Routledge.

Goodin, D. & Yoshitake, D. (1998, March 3). "Gates: Microsoft No Monopoly." ABC News. Available: http://www.abcnews.com

Goodnow, J., (1973, January). "Compensation arguments on conservation tasks." *Developmental Psychology.*

Greenberg, M. H. (1996). *Future net.* New York: Mass Market Paperback.

Grey, V. (1997). *Web without a weaver: How the internet is shaping our future.* Concord, CA: Open Heart Press.

Group for the Advancement of Psychiatry, Committee on Social Issues. (1982). *The child and television drama: The psychosocial impact of cumulative viewing.* New York: Mental Health Materials Center.

Grove, A. (1996). *Only the paranoid survive: How to exploit the crisis points that challenge every company and career.* New York: Doubleday.

Gruen, E. (1995, October 25). "Defining the Digital Consumer" IV agenda: Digital Kids pre-conference seminar. New York.

Gunter, B. (1990). *Children and television: The one eyed monster?* New York: Routledge.

Hafner, K. (1995, January). "Adventures on-line." *Working Woman.* pp. 48–52, 77–78.

Holliday, J., (1995, October). "Response bias in children's judgments of sense of sentences." *Perceptual Motor Skills, 43.*

"Hot off the presses." (1997, June 16). *Interactive Week,* p. 8.

Interactive Marketing News. (1995, November 10). "Children get growing online attention."

Internet Strategic Communications. (1988). Juno and IDI announce Internet lobbying alliance. [On-line] Available: http://idi.net

Jackson, T. (1997). *Inside Intel: Andy Grove and the rise of the world's most powerful chip company.* New York: Penguin-Putnam.

Jacobson, M. F. (1995). *Marketing madness: A survival guide for a consumer society.* Boulder, CO: Westview Press.

Jones, D. B. (1988). *Children's media market place.* New York: Neil-Schuman.

Jordan, A. (1996). *The state of children's television: An examination of quantity, quality and industry beliefs.* (Annenberg Public Policy Center Report No. 2.) Philadelphia: University of Pennsylvania.

Jordan, A. & Sullivan, J. (1997). *Children's educational television regulations and the local broadcaster: Impact and implementation.* (Annenberg Public Policy Center Report No. 13). Philadelphia:

University of Pennsylvania.

Journal of Business Research. (1974, October). "The effects of cognitive development on children's responses to television advertising."

Kantrowitz, B. (1994, May 16). "Men, women, and computers." *Newsweek.* pp. 48–55.

Kline, S. (1993). *Out of the garden: Toys, TV, and children's culture in the age of marketing.* New York: Verso.

Kunkel, D. & Gantz, W. (1992). "Children's television advertising in the multichannel environment." *Journal of Communication, 42.* 134–153.

Kunkel, D. & Roberts, D. (1991). "Young minds and marketplace values: Issues in children's television advertising." *Journal of Social Issues, 47.* 57–72.

Levine, M. (1996). *Viewing violence: How media violence affects your child's and adolescent's development.* New York: Doubleday.

Levinson, P. (1997). *The soft edge: A natural history and future of the information revolution.* New York: Routledge.

Liebert, R. & Sprafkin, J. (1988). *The early window: Effects of television on children and youth.* New York: Pergamon.

Lyons, C. (1998). *The new censors: Movies and the culture wars.* Philadelphia, PA: Temple University Press. Available: Hyperlink http://temple.edu/tempress/titles/1219   http://temple.edu/tempress/titles/1219reg.html

Maccoby, E. (1964). "Effects of the mass media." In M. L. Hoffman, & L. W. Hoffman (Eds.), *Review of child development research* (Vol. 1). New York: Russell Sage Foundation.

McChesney, R. W. (1993). *Telecommunications, mass media, and democracy: The battle for the control of U.S. broadcasting, 1928–1935.* New York: Oxford University Press.

McLuhan, M. (1967). *The medium is the message.* New York: Bantam Books.

McLuhan, M. (1989). *The global village: Transformations in world life and media in the 21st century.* New York: Oxford University Press.

McLuhan, M (1995). *Essential McLuhan.* New York: Basic Books.

McNeal, J. U. (1964). *Children as consumers. Bureau of Business Research,* Austin, Texas: The University of Texas at Austin.

McNeal, J. U. (1969). "The child consumer: A new market." *Journal of Retailing, 40.*

Meringoff, L. (1980). *Children and advertising: An annotated bibliog-*

raphy. New York: Children's Advertising Review Unit, National Advertising Division, Council of Better Business Bureaus.

Minow, N., & LaMay, C.L. (1995) *Abandoned in the wasteland: Children, television, and the First Amendment.* New York: Hill & Wang.

Montgomery, K. C. (1996, July–August). "Children in the Digital Age." *American Prospect,* [On-line serial], 27. Available: http://epn.org/prospect/27/27/mont.html

National Telecommunications and Information Administration (1995). *Falling through the net: A survey of the "have-nots" in rural and urban America.* Washington, DC: U.S. Department of Commerce.

Negroponte, N. (1995). *Being digital.* New York: Random House.

Nisbett, R. E., & Wilson, T. D. (1977, May). "Telling more than we know: Verbal reports on mental processes." *Psychological Review,* 84.

Noah, T. (1996, April 4). "Advertising: Study says minors respond more to cigarette ads than do adults." *Wall Street Journal.*

Packard, V. (1971). "The ad and the id." In F. Rissover & D. C. Birch (Eds.), *Mass media and the popular arts.* New York: McGraw-Hill.

Palmer, E. (1988). *Television and America's children: A crisis of neglect.* New York: Oxford University Press.

Palmer, E. L. & Dorr, A. (Eds.) (1980). *Children and the faces of television: Teaching, violence, and selling.* New York: Academic Press.

Patrick, W. (1988). *The FDA.* New York: Chelsea House.

Paul, G. S. (1996). *Beyond humanity: Cyberevolution and future minds.* Boston, M.A. Charles River Media.

Pember, D. (1993). *Mass media law.* Dubuque, IA: Brown & Benchmark.

Piaget, J. (1965). *The child's conception of the world.* Totowa, NJ: Littlefield, Adams.

Piaget, J. (1971). *Biology and knowledge.* Chicago: University of Chicago Press.

Piaget, J. (1972). *The psychology of the child.* New York: Basic Books.

Piaget, J. (1987). *The construction of the child's reality.* Cambridge, MA: Cambridge University Press.

Piller, C., (1994, September). "Consumers want more than TV overload from the information superhighway, but will they get it?" *MacWorld.*

Polly, J. (1996). *The internet kids and family yellow pages.* Berkeley,

CA: Osborne McGraw-Hill.

"Printers' ink." (1897, August 25). *Harper's Weekly.* Vol. 20, p. 42.

Quittner, J. (1995, April 3). "Vice raid on the net." *Time.* 63.

Reed, R., & Reed, M. (1992). *The encyclopedia of television, cable and video.* New York: Van Nostrand Reinhold.

Renaissance C National Research Council. (1994). *Realizing the information future: The internet and beyond.* Washington, DC: National Academy Press.

Robertson, D. S. (1998). *The new Renaissance: Computers and the next level of civilization.* New York: Oxford University Press.

Roman, J. (1996). *Love, light, and a dream — Television's past, present, and future.* Westport, CT: Praeger.

Rosen, P. T. (1980). *The modern Stentors: Radio broadcasting and the federal government.* Westport, CT: Greenwood Press.

Ross, L. (1995). *Netlaw: Your rights in the online world.* CA: McGraw-Hill.

Rubenstein, E. A., et al. (Eds.). (1975). *Television in day-to-day life: Patterns of use.* (Reports and papers, Vol. IV; Technical Report to the Surgeon General's Scientific Advisory Committee on Television and Social Behavior). Rockville, MD: National Institute of Mental Health.

Schramm, W., Lyle, J. & Parker, E. B. (1961). *Television in the lives of our children.* Palo Alto, CA: Stanford University Press.

Schramm, W. (1971). *The process and effects of mass communication.* Urbana: University of Illinois Press.

Seiter, E. (1993). *Sold separately: Children and parents in consumer culture.* New Brunswick, NJ: Rutgers University Press.

Signorielli, N. (1991). *A sourcebook on children and television.* New York: Greenwood Press.

Smith, L. J. (1994). "A content analysis of gender differences in children's advertising." *Journal of Broadcasting & Electronic Media,* 38. 323–37.

Stanger, J. (1997). *Television in the home: 1997 national survey of parents and children.* (Annenberg Public Policy Center Survey Series No. 2). Philadelphia: University of Pennsylvania.

Starek, R. (1997, July 25). The ABC's at the FTC: Marketing and advertising to children [On-line]. Available: http://www.ftc.gov/speeches/starek/minnfin.html

Stone, R. A. (1995). *The war of desire and technology at the close of the mechanical age.* Cambridge, MA: MIT Press.

Street, L. F. (1997). *Law of the internet.* Charlottesville, VA: Lexis Law Publishers.

Talbott, S. L. (1995). *The future does not compute: Transcending the machines in our midst.* Sebastopol, CA: O'Reilly & Associates.

Turkle, S. (1995). *Life on the screen: Identity in the age of the internet.* New York: Simon & Schuster.

Turner, E. S. (1953). *The shocking history of advertising.* New York: E.P. Dutton.

United States, Congress, Senate, Committee on Commerce, Science, and Transportation. (1989). *Children's television act of 1989.* Washington, DC: U.S. Government Printing Office.

United States, Congress, Senate, Committee on Commerce, Science, and Transportation. (1996). *Telecommunications act of 1996.* Washington, DC: U.S. Government Printing Office.

Wackman, D. B., & Ward, S. (1976). "The developmental theory and research and the implications for research on children's responses to television." *Comunication Research.*

Wallace, J., & Mangan, M. (1996). *Sex, laws & cyberspace.* New York: M & T Books.

Ward, S. (1971). *Effects of television advertising on children and adolescents.* (Marketing Science Institute Report). Cambridge, MA: Harvard University Press.

Ward, S. (1972). "Advertising and youth: Two studies." *Sloan Management Review* 14. pp. 63–82.

Ward, S. & Wackman, D. B. (1971). "Television advertising and intrafamily influence: Children's purchase influence attempts and parental yielding." In E. A. Rubinstein, G. A. Comstock, & J. P. Murray (Eds.), *Television and social behavior: Vol. 4. Television in day-to-day life: Patterns of use.* Washington, DC: U.S. Department of Health, Education, and Welfare.

Ward, S., & Wackman, D. B. (1973). "Children's information processing of television advertising." In P. Clarke (Ed.), *New models for mass communication research.* Beverly Hills, CA: Sage.

Ward, S., Wackman, D. B., & Wartella, E. (1975). *Children learning to buy: The development of consumer information processing skills* (Marketing Science Institute Report). Cambridge, MA: Harvard University Press.

Wartella, E., & Ettema, J. S. (1976, January). "A cognitive develop-

mental study of children's attention to television commercials."
Communication Research, 1. p. 69–88.

Williamson, J. (1978). *Decoding advertisements.* New York: Marion
Boyars.

Yang, E. (1998). Why congress wants to talk to microsoft [On-line].
Available: http://www.idg.net/docids/Microsoft/Congress/antitrust/
rumblings/industry

Young, B. M. (1990). *Television advertising and children.* Oxford,
England: Clarendon Press.

Index